The Ultimate Hockey
Quiz Book

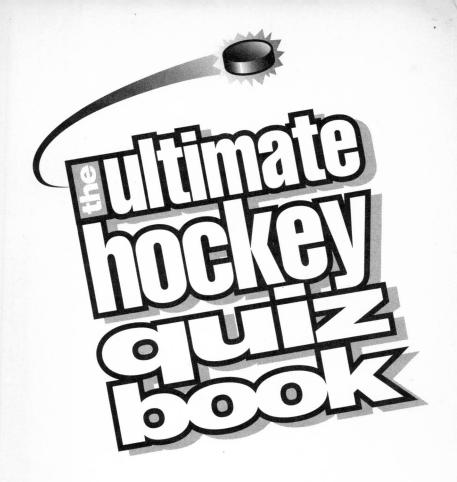

the ultimate hockey quiz book

Brian McFarlane

KEY PORTER BOOKS

Photo credits: Brian McFarlane p. 58, 63, 114; Canapress p.8, 23, 28, 109, 151

Canadian Cataloguing in Publication Data

McFarlane, Brian, 1931-
The ultimate hockey quiz book

ISBN 1-55263-091-9

1. Hockey – Miscellanea. 2. National Hockey League – Miscellanea.
I. Title.

GV847.M33 1999   796.962   C99-931124-7

The publisher gratefully acknowledges the support of the Canada Council for the Arts and the Ontario Arts Council for its publishing program.

Canada

We acknowledge the financial support of the Government of Canada through the Book Publishing Industry Development Program (BPIDP) for our publishing activities.

Key Porter Books Limited
70 The Esplanade
Toronto, Ontario
Canada M5E 1R2

www.keyporter.com

Design and Electronic formatting: Lightfoot Art & Design Inc.

Printed and bound in Canada

00 01 02 03 6 5 4 3 2

This book is dedicated to the memory of a man who never played hockey. He never coached, managed or owned a team. He never refereed, wrote about or broadcast the game. He was an avid fan but he never even saw a Stanley Cup game. And yet he's an honored member of the Hockey Hall of Fame. It's up to you, clever reader, to identify him.

This book is dedicated to the memory of Lord Stanley of Preston.

Contents

Mike Modano's combination of speed and finesse were a big part of the Dallas Stars, 1999 Stanley Cup Win.

INTRODUCTION

I've been involved with hockey for as long as I can remember. As a young boy I skated wherever there was ice—on frozen ponds and creeks, at the local outdoor rink, even in the street. I listened to Foster Hewitt's play-by-play of Toronto Maple Leaf games every Saturday night and I dreamed of the day when I too would play in those great shrines of hockey—Maple Leaf Gardens, the Montreal Forum, the Detroit Olympia, the Boston Garden, the Chicago Stadium and Madison Square Garden in New York.

As I grew to manhood, my dreams of professional glory faded. Three years of play at the junior A level and four years of college hockey at St. Lawrence University failed to attract the interest of the pros. So I settled for second best, commenting on the game, first on *Hockey Night in Canada* and later on NBC, and later writing a number of books about the most exciting team sport I knew.

How fortunate I was to work with broadcasting legends like Foster and Bill Hewitt from their famous gondola at Maple Leaf Gardens, with Dick Irvin and Danny Gallivan from the Forum in Montreal, and with Tim Ryan and Ted Lindsay and Peter (hockey's most popular) Puck on the NBC telecasts in the mid-seventies.

My involvement with hockey as a broadcaster and author always took me to places where, inevitably, questions are asked by fans. How thick is that little puck? How many career goals did Gordie Howe score in the NHL? Can you name the NHL teams Wayne Gretzky has played for?

This book, listing hundreds of trivia questions about hockey and dozens of fascinating facts about the game, will test your knowledge of, and hopefully enhance your interest in, a sport that is now played in countries all around the world.

Some of the questions will be a snap for the true fan of the game, others are as tough as Tie Domi. I hope fans young and old, in places near and far, will enjoy and learn from what follows.

By they way, the puck is one inch thick (and three inches in circumference), Gordie Howe scored 801 career goals in the NHL and Wayne Gretzky played with four NHL clubs—Edmonton, Los Angeles, St. Louis and New York.

There's the whistle. You've got the puck and you're on your way.

Brian McFarlane

Hockey People

Identify the hockey personalities.

1. He wrote a best selling book about his life as a goalie in 1983.

2. He was a league executive who was accused of trying to get himself inducted into the Hockey Hall of Fame in 1993.

3. He's the only "honored member" to resign from the Hockey Hall of Fame.

4. She was the first woman executive to have her name engraved on the Stanley Cup.

5. He was the eccentric coach who guided Philadelphia to back-to-back Stanley Cups in the mid-seventies.

6. He made a brief comeback during the 1997–98 season in order to claim he played pro hockey in six decades.

7. He quit the Winnipeg Jets to embark on a successful major league baseball career.

8. He was the original owner of the Los Angeles Kings.

9. He became the first player in NHL history to retire after winning the league's scoring title.

10. In 1947, he tinkered with a Jeep engine and the front end of two cars to invent a machine that is now synonymous with good ice.

11. He was pro hockey's only playing grandfather in the late seventies.

12. In 1978, the Birmingham Bulls of the WHA decided not to sign this player after a number of season-ticket holders complained about the color of his skin.

13. This teenager still had three seasons of junior hockey eligibility left when the WHA's Indianapolis owner signed him to a seven-year personal services contract for a reported $1.7 million.

14. In 1995, he became the first player from Sweden to capture the Calder Trophy.

15. All three of the NHL clubs he's coached are known as "original six" franchises and he's won coach-of-the-year honors with them all.

Answers:

1. Ken Dryden, 2. Gil Stein, 3. Alan Eagleson, 4. Marguerite Norris. In 1989, Sonia Scurfield, co-owner of the Calgary Flames, had her name inscribed on the Cup, as did Marie-Denise DeBartolo, President of the Pittsburgh Penguins, in 1991, and Marian Ilitch, co-owner of the Detroit Red Wings, in 1997 and 1998. 5. Fred Shero, 6. Gordie Howe, 7. Kirk McKaskill, 8. Jack Kent Cooke, 9. Mario Lemieux, 10. Frank Zamboni, 11. Gordie Howe, 12. Tony McKegney, 13. Wayne Gretzky, 14. Peter Forsberg, 15. Pat Burns.

Tragedy and Near Tragedy

1. On March 22, 1989, this goalie suffered a frightening neck injury during a game in Buffalo. A skate blade slashed the goalie's neck and severed his jugular vein. Several spectators fainted when they saw blood spurting from the wound and the telecast team refused to show replays of the incident. The goalie made a complete recovery. Can you name him?

2. This current NHL star was with New Jersey when, in the off season, he had his left thumb severed in a farm accident. He was rushed to hospital where the thumb was reattached by surgeons who gave him a 50–50 chance of ever playing again. He came back the following season to score goals in six consecutive games, setting a club record. He is _____.

3. This Hartford Whaler was seriously injured during the 1980–81 season when he impaled himself on the metal puck deflector in the middle of the goal net. The metal penetrated his buttock to a depth of almost six inches and doctors said he was half an inch away from

becoming an invalid. He made an astonishing recovery and enjoyed a 16-year career in the NHL. Can you name him?

4. Eight months after undergoing brain surgery, this forward scored three goals in the second game of his dramatic comeback with San Jose. His sister was a star player on the 1998 U.S. Olympic team. He is _____.

5. Following Detroit's Stanley Cup victory in 1997, this star Red Wing defenseman was critically injured in a limo accident. He is

_____.

6. The only player to die as the result of an injury in a game was a member of the Minnesota North Stars. One of hockey's most coveted trophies is named after him. Name the player.

7. A Boston rookie's career ended suddenly one October night in the 1982–83 season. The player suffered a brain hemorrhage during a game against Vancouver. The player survived but permanent brain damage resulted. "He was going to be a great star," said teammate Terry O'Reilly. Can you name the Bruin rookie?

8. In 1969, a vicious stick-swinging duel between a Boston Bruin tough guy and a St. Louis forward resulted in an injury to the Bruin that required a five-hour brain operation. Who were the two players involved?

9. In the early hours of the morning of February 21, 1974, following a game in Toronto, a veteran NHL defenseman was killed when his Italian-made sports car crashed near St. Catharines, Ontario. Can you name this Hall of Famer?

10. On January 4, 1975, Boston's Dave Forbes butt-ended a popular Minnesota player in the eye with his stick and was suspended by league President Clarence Campbell for 10 games. Forbes was also charged with aggravated assault. If found guilty, he could have faced five to 10 years in prison. The victim sued for $3.5 million but five years later the case was settled out of court for an undisclosed sum. Who was the Minnesota player?

11. During the 1978–79 season, Wilf Paiement clubbed a Detroit player in the face with his stick and was punished with a 15-game suspension and a $500 fine. But the Detroit player sued and won a settlement of close to $1 million. Who was he?

12. In 1933, Boston's Eddie Shore struck a Toronto player from behind, fracturing his skull. Shore was suspended for 16 games. Who was the Leaf player who suffered the career-ending injury?

13. On March 24, 1981, this Montreal superstar, known for his high speed driving, fell asleep at the wheel of his car and rammed into a fence. A metal post sliced off part of his ear. Had the player's head been an inch or two to the right he would have been killed. Can you name him?

14. On November 10, 1985, after celebrating his team's 10th straight victory, this popular goaltender was killed when he drove his sports car into a retaining wall at high speed. His death was said to be alcohol-related. Can you name him?

15. During the 1970–71 season, the father of this rookie player was furious when he was unable to see his son being interviewed on *Hockey Night in Canada*. He grabbed a rifle, drove to a nearby TV station and demanded the station carry the game in which his son was playing. A shootout with police resulted and the man was killed. Can you name the player? Can you name the player's father?

16. He was a star defenseman for the Philadelphia Flyers when they captured the Stanley Cup in 1974. Diagnosed with leukemia, he died in mid-May of 1977. Who was he?

17. He was killed in a small plane crash in the summer of 1951. His last hurrah in hockey was scoring the Stanley Cup–winning goal in the '51 finals against Montreal. Who was he?

18. In 1950, he suffered a serious head injury during a playoff game in Detroit and was rushed to hospital where a small hole was drilled into his skull to relieve the pressure. The surgeon who operated said if another 30 minutes had passed it might have been too late to

save the player's life. The player recovered and went on to set team and league scoring records. Who was he?

19. This 54-year-old former NHL player turned sportscaster was shot and killed by a crazed gunman outside a TV studio in Ottawa in 1995. Can you name him?

20. In 1995, this 50-year-old former NHL star went public with a medical . diagnosis indicating he had full-blown AIDS. Who was he?

Answers:

1. Clint Malarchuk, 2. Pat Verbeek, 3. Mark Howe, 4. Tony Granato, 5. Vladimir Konstantinov, 6. Bill Masterton, 7. Norman Leveille, 8. Ted Green and Wayne Maki, 9. Tim Horton, 10. Henry Boucha, 11. Dennis Polonich, 12. Ace Bailey, 13. Guy Lafleur, 14. Pelle Lindbergh, 15. Brian and Roy Spencer, 16. Barry Ashbee, 17. Bill Barilko, 18. Gordie Howe, 19. Brian Smith, 20. Bill Goldsworthy.

Name the Players

1. Here's a tough one. Can you name three NHL players, past or present, whose surnames can be spelled either frontwards or backwards?
   First clue: Two of the names have five letters, one has four letters.
   Second clue: One played three seasons with the Philadelphia Flyers, another played seven seasons with Vancouver, the third played 10 seasons with Calgary.

2. Can you name three players who played in more than 50 NHL games whose last name begins with the letter Q?

3. Can you name all three members of Buffalo's French Connection Line?

4. How about the members of Montreal's famous Punch Line?

5. In 1994, at the age of 21, he was named the youngest captain in the history of the Philadelphia Flyers. Who is he?

6. Can you name three goaltenders of the Jewish faith who played in the NHL?

7. Can you name the left winger who compiled back-to-back 54-and 55-goal seasons in 1991–92 and 1992–93 while playing on a line with Mario Lemieux?

8. Can you name all six of the Sutter brothers who played in the NHL?

9. Can you name the only Sutter brother who did not play in the NHL?

10. What is Wayne Gretzky's father's first name?

11. Few big league goalies have had surnames beginning with the letter P. Jacques Plante was one. Can you name two current NHL goalies whose surnames begin with P?

12. Can you name the first female player to be given a tryout by an NHL club? With which NHL club did she try out?

Answers:

1. Our palindromic playmakers are Gary Lupul, Joel Otto and Jiri Latal, 2. Quinn (Pat and Dan), Quintal, Quackenbush (Bill and Max), Quinney, Quint, Quilty and Quenneville, 3. Gilbert Perreault, Richard Martin and Rene Robert, 4. Toe Blake, Rocket Richard and Elmer Lach, 5. Eric Lindros, 6. Mike Veisor, Bernie Wolfe and Ross Brooks. Phil Stein (1 game) would be a fourth and Moe Roberts (10 games) a fifth, 7. Kevin Stevens, 8. Brian, Darryl, Duane, Rich, Brent, Ron, 9. Gary, 10. Walter, 11. Puppa, Potvin, 12. Manon Rheaume, Tampa Bay.

The ONly ONe

1. I'm the only player to score 30 or more goals in the NHL for 15 consecutive seasons.

2. I was a hot scorer too. I scored 50 or more goals every season for nine straight years. Now I'm in the Hockey Hall of Fame.

3. When I was in my prime I outscored everybody. One season I broke my pal Bobby Hull's single season record of 58 goals by scoring 76. You won't believe this, but in Junior B hockey I lost the scoring title in my league to Terry Crisp. And I remain the only player to take 550 shots on goal in one season.

4. I hated those prolific goal scorers—unless they were on my team. They didn't make life easy for me. I'm the only goaltender in seven decades to compile 15 shutouts in a season. I did it in 1969–70.

5. I'm the only player to be assessed 67 minutes in penalties in one game. Funny thing is, all my penalties took place in the first period of a game between the Kings and the Flyers. I never did like those Flyers.

6. I'm the player who showed up for and played in a record 920 consecutive NHL games. My streak ended in 1987.

7. Surely you remember me. I played in six different cities in the WHA, and I'm the only player in that league to score almost 800 points. I finished with a record 798.

8. None of the NHL record books list my rare achievement but I'm proud to be the only player to perform for all six of the Original Six NHL clubs. Because this is one of the toughest questions in this book, I'll give you a hint. My initials are V.L.

9. You're all too young to have seen me play but I'm still the only NHLer to score seven goals in a game. I did it against Toronto back in 1920.

10. I played long before the NHL was formed and I was a star despite being blind in one eye. I'm the only player to score 14 goals in a playoff game for the Stanley Cup. The young whippersnappers playing today will never top that record.

11. I'm the only U.S.-born player to score over 500 goals in my career.

12. I'm the only NHL goaltender to play in 79 games during the regular season.

13. I'm the only European player to lead the NHL in scoring. I did it first in 1994–95.

14. I'm the only Hart Trophy winner whose father also won the award.

15. I'm the only NHL player to score 20 or more goals with six different teams in the league. Here's a clue: I scored 52 goals for Detroit in 1993–94.

16. I'm the only man who served as president of the NHL who is not in the Hockey Hall of Fame. Who am I?

17. I've been around so long (over 30 years) that I've become the only general manager in NHL history to guide my team to over 1,000 victories.

18. I'm the only hockey personality who has a dog that's almost as famous as I am. Everybody knows me but what's my dog's name?

19. I'm the only NHL goaltender to collect three points (all assists) in one game. I did it for the Calgary Flames on Feb. 10, 1993, in a 13–1 rout of San Jose. Who am I?

Answers:

1. Mike Gartner, 2. Mike Bossy, 3. Phil Esposito, 4. Tony Esposito, 5. Randy Holt, 6. Doug Jarvis, 7. Andre Lacroix, 8. Vic Lynn, 9. Joe Malone, 10. One-Eyed Frank McGee, 11. Joey Mullen, 12. Grant Fuhr, 13. Jaromir Jagr, 14. Brett Hull, 15. Ray Sheppard, 16. Gil Stein. Garry Bettman is not in the Hall but he rules as NHL Commissioner, 17. Harry Sinden, 18. Blue (Don Cherry's dog), 19. Jeff Reese.

Trophies and Awards

Hockey gives out many trophies every year and it's difficult to keep track of what each represents. It's your job to match the trophy with its significance.

1.	Ross	a.	Best goaltender
2.	Vezina	b.	Top rookie
3.	Adams	c.	Best defenseman

4.	Masterton	d.	MVP of playoffs
5.	Norris	e.	Top goal scorer
6.	Hart	f.	NHL's leading scorer
7.	Calder	g.	Coach of the year
8.	Lady Byng	h.	Perseverance, sportsmanship, dedication
9.	Richard	i.	Most valuable to his team
10.	Smythe	j.	Sportsmanship and gentlemanly conduct

Answers:

1. -f, 2. -a, 3. -g, 4. -h, 5. -c, 6. -i, 7. -b, 8. -j, 9. -e, 10. -d.

It takes a real hockey expert to know the significance of these lesser-known trophies and awards.

1.	Jennings Trophy	a.	For service to hockey in the U.S.
2.	Lester Pearson Award	b.	For finishing first overall
3.	Bud Ice Award	c.	Best goals-against average
4.	President's Trophy	d.	Leader in plus-minus stats
5.	Lester Patrick Trophy	e.	Outstanding player as selected by NHLPA

Answers:

1.-c, 2.-e, 3.-d, 4.-b, 5.-a.

Speaking of Trophies . . .

1. How many major individual trophies has Wayne Gretzky won?
   a. 15–20 b. 20–25 c. 35–40

2. Some great young scorers were drafted in 1971—Guy Lafleur, Marcel Dionne and Richard Martin. But a player who had performed in the NHL in the previous season captured the Calder Trophy in 1971–72. Can you name him?

3. Only three players have won the scoring title and the Lady Byng Trophy in the same season. And two of them did it twice. Can you name them?

4. Who won back-to-back Hart trophies in 1997 and 1998?

5. True or false? Eric Lindros has never won the Hart Trophy.

6. True or false? A goalie has never won the Lady Byng Trophy for gentlemanly conduct.

7. Who was the first defenseman to win the Lady Byng?

8. The Montreal Canadiens have had two Lady Byng winners. Toe Blake was one. Who was the other?

9. Who was the last Toronto Maple Leaf player to win the Art Ross Trophy as NHL scoring champion?

10. Only one NHL star has captured the Ross, Hart and Lady Byng trophies in consecutive years. Can you name him?

11. If two players finish tied in points for the scoring lead at the end of the season, who gets the Art Ross Trophy?

12. Name the only player who won a major NHL trophy so often he got to keep it.

13. In the decade of the eighties, three different goalies captured the Conn Smythe Trophy as MVP of the playoffs. Can you name them?

14. True or false? The Edmonton Oilers captured the Stanley Cup four times in the eighties. Each time they did it, Glen Sather won the Adams Trophy as coach of the year.

15. The silver bowl atop the Stanley Cup is the original one. True or false?

Answers:

1. *c. Wayne has won 37 major individual trophies.*
2. *It was goalie Ken Dryden. Dryden was eligible for the award even though he'd played half a dozen games the season before and had won the Conn Smythe Trophy as MVP of the 1971 playoffs. It was a tough break for Martin, who scored a (then) record 44 goals as a Sabre rookie.*
3. *In 1938, Gordon Drillon of the Leafs won both awards. In 1967 and again in 1968, Stan Mikita of Chicago captured both trophies. Wayne Gretzky won both in 1991 and 1994.*

4. **Dominik Hasek of the Buffalo Sabres.**
5. **False. Lindros won the Hart Trophy in 1995.**
6. **True. No goalie has ever won the Lady Byng.**
7. **The first defenseman to win the Lady Byng was Detroit's Bill Quackenbush in 1949. Before Quackenbush, 24 forwards had captured it.**
8. **Mats Naslund.**
9. **Gordon Drillon, back in 1938.**
10. **Stan Mikita of Chicago did it in 1967 and 1968.**
11. **The player with the most goals. That's how Marcel Dionne captured the crown over Wayne Gretzky in 1980. Both had 137 points but Dionne scored 53 goals to Gretzky's 51.**
12. **Frank Boucher of the New York Rangers. Boucher is the only player who so monopolized an individual award that it was finally given to him to keep. After Boucher won the Lady Byng Trophy for sportsmanship seven times in eight years he was allowed to keep the original.**
13. **Billy Smith (1983), Patrick Roy (1986), Ron Hextall (1987).**
14. **False. He won it once, in 1986.**
15. **False. Several years ago the NHL had the original bowl replaced with a duplicate. It seems that Lord Stanley's gift to hockey was in danger of cracking. To guarantee its survival, a substitute bowl was fashioned. The original Stanley Cup is now safe in the Hockey Hall of Fame.**

Who Am I?

1. I'm the only non–Montreal Canadien to have my name engraved on the Stanley Cup eight times—four with my first club and four more with my second. Who am I?

2. Many years ago I coached the Philadelphia Flyers to a record that still stands—35 games without a loss. We lost a game in the first week of the season and didn't lose another until January 7 in Minnesota when our record was 26–1–10. Who am I?

3. You're not going to believe this but I'm a goaltender who compiled a record of 12–47–7 in 1953–54. My team finished dead last and I surrendered 213 goals in 66 games. My goals-against average went from 2.50 to 3.23 that season. But guess what? They awarded me the Hart Trophy as league MVP. It was the biggest surprise of my life. Who am I?

4. I broke in as a forward with the Montreal Canadiens in 1969–70 and

expected to make a lot of money in playoff bonuses. But the Habs missed the playoffs that season. I was traded to Detroit during the following season and later played with Kansas City and Washington—all weak clubs. As a result, I'm the only player to perform in 734 NHL games who never got to play in a playoff game. Who am I?

5. As a coach I couldn't have asked for more. In the 1993 playoffs my team won 10 overtime games. My team lost an overtime game in the first round against Quebec, then won two overtime contests against the Nordiques. We went on to win 10 more overtime games; three in four games against Buffalo, and two more in a five-game series against the Islanders. In the finals against Los Angeles, we won three more games requiring extra play and captured the Stanley Cup. Who am I?

6. In the WHA, I didn't have the charisma of Bobby Hull or Frank Mahovlich, two Hall of Famers. But I outscored both those men and everybody else who played in the league. In fact, I'm the only WHA player to amass 798 points and I did it in six different cities. Who am I?

7. I learned to play hockey on roller skates in New York City and somehow became skilled enough to play in over 1,000 NHL games and score 502 career goals—a record for an American-born player. Who am I?

8. I won the Hobey Baker Award in 1993 as the top U.S. college player and was drafted fourth overall later that year. I scored only 39 points in my rookie NHL season then jumped to 50 goals and 108 points as a sophomore in 1995–96. What a nice surprise. I even made the first All-Star Team and won the Lady Byng Trophy that year. Who am I?

9. Shortly after my team selected me as the No. 1 pick at the 1998 draft, the team owner started predicting a Hall of Fame berth for me. He said I'd become "the Michael Jordan of hockey." Talk about putting pressure on a guy. Do you know who I am?

10. In 1998, I was 65 years old and I had my name engraved on the Stanley Cup for the eighth time. And not once as a player. Who am I?

11. On January 2, 1999, I joined Billy Smith, Ron Hextall, Chris Osgood

and Martin Brodeur as the only goal-scoring goaltenders in the NHL. But I'm the only one to score a goal and earn a shutout in the same game. Who am I?

12. Nobody seemed to notice, but my scoring exploits during the eighties were second only to Wayne Gretzky (1,864 points to 1,024). And my brothers played better hockey than his brothers. I was inducted into the Hall of Fame in 1998. Who am I?

13. Speaking of brothers, I followed my two older brothers into the Hockey Hall of Fame in 1998. We're the only brother threesome in the Hall. Can you name us?

14. I retired with 601 career goals (ninth highest in history) and 1,398 points (most ever by a European player). Not bad for a player drafted in the third round (69th overall) in 1980. I also played on five Stanley Cup winners. Who am I?

15. Head injuries forced me into retirement in 1998. I left the NHL as the third highest scoring American-born player behind Joey Mullen and Phil Housley. Who am I?

Answers:

1. Red Kelly, 2. Pat Quinn, 3. Al Rollins, 4. Guy Charron, 5. Jacques Demers, 6. Andre Lacroix, 7. Joe Mullen, 8. Paul Kariya, 9. Vincent Lecavalier, 10. Coach Scotty Bowman, 11. Damian Rhodes, Ottawa, in a 6–0 win over New Jersey. 12. Peter Stastny, 13. Charlie, Lionel and Roy Conacher, 14. Jari Kurri, 15. Pat LaFontaine.

(More) Who Am I?

1. In 1980, I became the first hockey player to skate with an Olympic gold-medal–winning team and a Stanley Cup–winning team—in the same season. I went on to play with three more Stanley Cup winners. Who am I?

2. I was on that same Olympic team in 1980. In fact, no player on that club got more attention than I did. The pro team I signed with after the Olympics gave me $85,000 and hoped I would save the franchise.

During the 1994-95 season, Jaromir Jagr became the first
European player to lead the NHL in scoring.

Coca-Cola gave me another $35,000 to do a commercial. But my big-league career never took off and I soon faded from the hockey scene. Who am I?

3. During the 1988–89 season, I scored five goals in a game and I scored them in five different ways—even strength, short-handed, power play, penalty shot and empty net. They say it's never been done before. But then, I did a lot of things that have never been done before. Who am I?

4. One of the biggest mistakes the Rangers made back in 1976 was trading me to Boston. I really caught fire after that and enjoyed many great seasons with my new team. I finished my career in 1988 with 448 goals. Who am I?

5. I'm a coach with one of the great teams in hockey. In my former job, I wore a uniform but not a hockey uniform. In that job, a guy came looking for me once. Wanted to shoot me. And a lady hit me over the head with a turkey one time. I'm much happier where I am and I thank Wayne Gretzky for suggesting I try for a career in the NHL. Who am I?

6. What a thrill it was to be selected first overall in the entry draft of 1983—the first U.S. player to be chosen No. 1. A center, I scored only 10 goals in my rookie season and some people say I never lived up to my potential. I'm the only NHLer born in New Brunswick, N.J. Who am I?

7. Vancouver gave up on me too soon. Said I had a bad attitude. Well, I showed them—I went on to score 50 goals or more three times with my new team and I was named team captain. Unfortunately, I had problems with management there and lost my captaincy. I was traded twice after that. Who am I?

8. In 1984, I was runner-up to Tom Barrasso as Rookie of the Year. I'm the youngest player ever to appear in an All-Star game and I was only 21 when I was named captain of my team. I hold the team record for the fastest 50 goals in my team's history. Who am I?

9. I've done well for a guy who was drafted out of Clarkson College as the 210th player selected. They tell me I'm the highest scoring ex-college player in NHL history … and I played on one of the NHL's greatest lines a few years ago. Who am I?

10. Now retired, I played a tough position and was known for my mean disposition. Look at my career penalty minutes—almost 500 minutes (482). That's got to be a record for my position. I won a couple of major awards and my name is on the Stanley Cup in four places. By now, you must know who I am.

11. In my first year as a pro—in the minors—I scored a rookie record 50 goals in 67 games. I was born in Belleville, Ontario, and played junior hockey in Penticton, where I scored 105 goals in my first season. I was drafted in 1984 but well down the list (117th) and now I'm with my third NHL club. Both my dad and my uncle played with Chicago in the NHL. Who am I?

12. In 1992–93 I became the first Toronto Maple Leaf player since Dave Keon to win a major NHL award when I captured the Frank Selke Trophy as best defensive forward. I've had a great career for someone who was drafted 134th overall from the Cornwall juniors in 1982. I'm one of Don Cherry's pets. Who am I?

Answers:
1. Ken Morrow, 2. Jim Craig, 3. Mario Lemieux, 4. Rick Middleton, 5. Pat Burns, former policeman, 6. Brian Lawton, 7. Rick Vaive, 8. Steve Yzerman, 9. Dave Taylor, 10. Billy Smith, 11. Brett Hull, 12. Doug Gilmour.

Who Said It?

Hockey people say the darnedest things. Here are some famous quotes. You figure out who said them.

1. "Them Penguins are done like dinner."

2. "We can't win at home and we can't win on the road and my problem as a coach is I can't think of anywhere else we can play."

3. "It's a cannonading shot!"

4. "They are putting a Mickey Mouse operation on the ice."

5. "My ex-wife made me a millionaire. Of course, I started out with three million."

6. "Have another donut, you fat pig."

7. "If you can't beat 'em in the alley, you can't beat 'em on the ice."

8. "He shoots, he scores!"

Answers:

1. *Tiger Williams. His famous "done like dinner" quote was said to the author during a* Hockey Night in Canada *interview when Tiger and the Toronto Maple Leafs were playing the Pittsburgh Penguins in the spring of 1976.*

2. *Harry Neale, former coach of the Vancouver Canucks, when his team suffered through a losing streak.*

3. *The late Montreal broadcasting great Danny Gallivan, famous for coining words like "cannonading" and "spinnerama."*

4. *Wayne Gretzky, to describe the New Jersey Devils in 1983. Wayne later apologized to the Devils for his remarks.*

5. *Bobby Hull, after his divorce from wife Joanne.*

6. *Devils' coach Jim Schoenfeld, to referee Don Koharski, after a playoff game in 1988.*

7. *Conn Smythe, founder of the Toronto Maple Leaf franchise.*

8. *Foster Hewitt, hockey's most famous broadcaster.*

Remember These Other Quotes?

1. After performing a first-ever feat in 1987, the goalie who accomplished it said: "It's really surprising, when you think of it, that nobody has done it before." Who was the goalie? What was he talking about?

2. In 1998, general manager Bob Clarke said, "If you want to be the highest paid player in the game or close to it, you've got to play that way. You're not a kid anymore." Who was he talking to?

3. A controversial message flashed across the scoreboard over center ice. It read: "Remember Korean Airlines flight 007. Don't cheer. Just boo." Who was responsible for these words?

4. Before this colorful chap became a TV star, he was dismissed as coach of a team that had a rocky start in the NHL. He said, "It's pretty hard to fly with eagles when you're mixed up with turkeys." Who was he? What team fired him?

5. In August of 1988, certain hockey fans called her everything from "Jezebel" to the "Yoko Ono of pro hockey." Who were they talking about and why?

6. After a bizarre playoff game on Mother's Day, 1988, the GM of the visiting team said: "We pulled three guys out of the stands and the difference between them and the guys we use every night was marginal." Who was the GM? What was he talking about?

7. After watching an opposing player sparkle in the 1988 playoffs, Boston coach Terry O'Reilly said, "He's the best, no doubt about it. There should be a league rule that he has to be passed around from team to team every year." Who was O'Reilly speaking of?

8. Before he made big headlines in Detroit, this troubled player said, "I've been having a few drinks here and there but that's my business." Name him.

9. Paul Coffey, one of his close friends, said with tears in his eyes, "There's no bloody way he wanted to go there." Go where? Who?

10. The team owner said of one of his Swedish players, "He could go into the corners with eggs in his pockets and not break any of them." Who was the owner? Who was he talking about?

11. During the 1967 playoffs, the Toronto coach sneered, "You can tell that junior B goaltender he won't be playing with a bunch of peashooters when he plays against us." Who was the coach? Who was the "junior B" goaltender?

An awesome physical presence, Eric Lindros is expected
to carry the mantle of superstardom following
Wayne Gretzky's retirement.

12. In 1962, during the All-Star break, this owner announced: "I have just signed Frank Mahovlich for one million dollars." Who was the owner? Did Frank ever play for his team?

Answers:

1. *Goalie Ron Hextall of Philadelphia, after scoring the first-ever goal by a goalie against the Boston Bruins.*
2. *Clarke was talking about Eric Lindros, who had suffered through a mediocre season.*
3. *Harold Ballard. The Leaf owner flashed the message to boo during an exhibition game in Toronto (featuring a Soviet team) after Korean Airlines flight 007 was shot down in 1983.*
4. *Don Cherry, uttered when he was fired as coach by the Colorado Rockies.*
5. *Janet Jones (Mrs. Wayne Gretzky), after Wayne was traded to L.A. Some fans blamed Janet for influencing Wayne to switch teams.*
6. *Boston GM Harry Sinden, talking about the use of substitute officials for the Mother's Day playoff game between Boston and New Jersey in 1988.*
7. *Wayne Gretzky, the Conn Smythe Trophy winner in 1988.*
8. *Detroit's Bob Probert.*
9. *Los Angeles. Wayne Gretzky.*
10. *Harold Ballard, discussing Swedish forward Inge Hammerstrom.*
11. *Punch Imlach, discussing Montreal's use of rookie goalie Rogie Vachon.*
12. *Chicago owner Jim Norris, who thought he'd purchased Mahovlich. The Leafs changed their minds about selling the Big M and Mahovlich never played for the Hawks.*

Oh Brother!

Part 1:

There have been many famous brother acts in the NHL. Your job is to fill in the name of the less famous brother.

1. Gordie and _____ Howe.
2. Chico and _____ Maki
3. Mickey and _____ Redmond
4. Denis and _____ Potvin
5. Neil, Paul and _____ Broten

6. Kevin and _____ Dineen
7. Wayne and _____ Gretzky
8. Kevin and _____ Hatcher
9. Ken and _____ Dryden
10. Joey and _____ Mullen
11. Pierre and _____ Turgeon
12. Eric and _____ Lindros
13. Mario and _____ Lemieux
14. Doug and _____ Wilson
15. Maurice and _____ Richard
16. Geoff and _____ Courtnall
17. Marcel and _____ Dionne
18. Bobby and _____ Hull
19. Pavel and _____ Bure
20. Frank and _____ Mahovlich

Part 2:

It will take a hockey expert to match up all of the following brother acts.

1. Lionel, Charlie and _____ Conacher
2. Max, Doug and _____ Bentley
3. Anton, Peter and _____ Stastny
4. Paul and _____ Cavallini
5. Andy and _____ Bathgate
6. Don and _____ Cherry
7. Odie and _____ Cleghorn
8. Nick and _____ Metz
9. Barclay, Bob and _____ Plager
10. Bill and _____ Quackenbush
11. Grant and _____ Warwick
12. Joe and _____ Watson
13. Dave and _____ Gardner
14. Larry and _____ Hillman
15. Bill and _____ Cook

Answers:
(Part 1)
1. Vic, 2. Wayne, 3 Dick, 4. Jean, 5. Aaron, 6. Gord or Peter, 7. Brent,
8. Derian, 9. Dave, 10. Brian, 11. Sylvain, 12. Brett, 13. Alain, 14. Murray,

Team Captains

1. Name five NHL captains, past and present, who were born outside of North America.

2. True or false? Bobby Orr was Boston's captain for three seasons in the seventies.

3. Name the Toronto captain who stripped the C off his jersey during the 1979–80 season to show his disdain for trades his team's general manager had made.

4. The youngest captain in Detroit Red Wing history was:
    a. Alex Delvecchio
    b. Gordie Howe
    c. Steve Yzerman

5. Name the captain who led the Philadelphia Flyers to back-to-back Stanley Cups in 1974 and '75.

6. Who holds the record as the longest serving captain in NHL history?

7. The second longest serving captain played for the same team as the player above (question 6). Can you name him?

8. This player was named team captain after being acquired from another NHL club in 1992. The deal included $15 million and a swap of several players. He won the Hart Trophy in 1995.

9. The captain of the Dallas Stars is:
    a. Mike Modano
    b. Derian Hatcher
    c. Bob Gainey

10. True or false? George Armstrong, Dave Keon, Darryl Sittler and Lanny McDonald all served as captains of the Toronto Maple Leafs.

Answers:

1. Yashin (Ottawa), Sundin (Toronto), Jagr (Pittsburgh), Mikita (Chicago) and P. Stastny (Quebec). 2. False. Orr was never a team captain. 3. Darryl Sittler, 4. Steve Yzerman, 5. Bobby Clarke, 6. Steve Yzerman, 7. Alex Delvecchio, 8. Eric Lindros, 9. Derian Hatcher, 10. McDonald was never a Leaf captain.

What's the Name Again?

Everyone knows that Rocket Richard's real first name was Maurice. But do you know the given names of the following NHL players?

1. Tiger Williams
2. Butch Goring
3. Spinner Spencer
4. King Clancy
5. Busher Jackson
6. Boom Boom Geoffrion
7. Red Kelly
8. Red Berenson
9. Dit Clapper
10. Butch Bouchard
11. Gump Worsley
12. Teeder Kennedy
13. Punch Imlach
14. Cat Francis
15. Bud Poile
16. Babe Pratt
17. Red Sullivan
18. Moose Vasko
19. Turk Broda
20. Red Horner
21. Bunny Larocque
22. Chuck Rayner
23. Chico Resch
24. Cowboy Flett
25. Toe Blake

Answers:

1. David, 2. Robert Thomas, 3. Brian, 4. Francis Michael, 5. Harvey, 6. Bernard, 7. Leonard, 8. Gordon, 9. Aubrey, 10. Emile, 11. Lorne, 12. Theodore (Ted), 13. George, 14. Emile, 15. Norman, 16. Walter, 17. George, 18. Elmer, 19. Walter, 20. Reginald, 21. Michel, 22. Claude Earl, 23. Glenn, 24. Bill, 25. Hector.

More Nicknames

Modern day hockey is devoid of colorful nicknames. Sure there's the Great One, Mario the Magnificent, the Russian Rocket and Eddie the Eagle. But where are Hambone and Fats, Goose and Bones, Porky and Applecheeks? Let's see you identify the following.

1. The Chicoutimi Cucumber
2. The Big M
3. The Big Train
4. Pocket Rocket
5. The Roadrunner
6. Little Beaver
7. Cyclone
8. Black Jack
9. Old Scarface
10. Old Poison
11. The Great Wall of China
12. Bootnose
13. Sweeney
14. Gentleman Joe
15. Flower
16. One-Eyed Frank
17. Goose
18. Bones
19. Jake the Snake
20. The Entertainer
21. Porky
22. Applecheeks
23. Fats
24. Slats
25. The Stratford Streak

Answers:

1. Georges Vezina, 2. Frank Mahovlich, 3. Lionel Conacher, 4. Henri Richard, 5. Yvan Cournoyer, 6. Marcel Dionne, 7. Fred Taylor, 8. Jack Stewart, 9. Ted Lindsay, 10. Nels Stewart, 11. Johnny Bower, 12. Sid Abel, 13. Dave Schriner, 14. Joe Primeau, 15. Guy Lafleur, 16. Frank McGee, 17. John McCormack, 18. Don Raleigh, 19. Jacques Plante, 20. Eddie Shack, 21. Woodrow Dumart, 22. Harry Lumley, 23. Alex Delvecchio, 24. Glen Sather, 25. Howie Morenz.

Find the Misfit

In the following groups, one name or word does not belong. It is a misfit.

1. Scotty Bowman, Al Arbour, Pat Burns, Lindy Ruff, Paul Stewart, Ken Hitchcock

2. Dave Williams, Dale Hunter, Tim Hunter, Paul Kariya, Marty McSorley, Chris Nilan

3. Mario Lemieux, Wayne Gretzky, Jaromir Jagr, Guy Lafleur, Bryan Trottier, Eric Lindros

4. Peter Forsberg, Mats Sundin, Brendan Shanahan, Ulf Samuelsson, Ulf Dahlen, Daniel Alfredsson

5. Bryan Berard, Joe Thornton, Chris Phillips, Ed Jovanovski, Mike Modano, Tie Domi

6. Avalanche, Penguins, Scouts, Bruins, Lightning, Panthers

7. Terry Gregson, Kerry Fraser, Paul Stewart, Don Koharski, John Ziegler, Bill McCreary

8. Fleet Center, National Car Rental Center, United Center, CoreStates Center, Hummingbird Center, General Motors Place

9. Charging, holding, hooking, skating, interference, high sticking

10. Yzerman, Lidstrom, Fedorov, Draper, Murphy, Ciccarelli

11. Frank Mahovlich, Dave Dryden, Dennis Hull, Tony Esposito, Brent Sutter, Vincent Damphousse

12. Scotty Bowman, Al Arbour, Mike Keenan, Kevin Constantine, Jacques Demers, Bob Johnson, Marc Crawford

13. John Davidson, Danny Gallivan, Howie Meeker, Dick Irvin, Jr., Foster Hewitt, Harold Ballard

14. Gordie Howe, Alex Delvecchio, Johnny Bucyk, Tim Horton, Doug Mohns, Dean Prentice, Harry Howell, Bob Gainey

15. Hart, Ross, Vezina, Norris, Smythe, Heisman

Answers:
1. *All are NHL coaches except Paul Stewart who is a referee.*
2. *All have over 3,000 penalty minutes except Kariya, a Lady Byng Trophy winner.*

3. *All have won the Art Ross trophy except for Lindros. Could also be all are Canadian-born except for Jagr.*
4. *All are Swedish players except for Shanahan.*
5. *All are number one draft selections except for Domi.*
6. *All are nicknames for current NHL clubs except for Scouts.*
7. *All are current NHL referees except for former NHL president John Ziegler.*
8. *All are names of NHL arenas except for the Hummingbird Centre.*
9. *All are infractions that can be penalized except for skating.*
10. *All were on back-to-back Stanley Cup winners in Detroit—except for Ciccarelli.*
11. *All had brothers who played in the NHL—except Damphousse.*
12. *All coached teams to the Stanley Cup—except for Kevin Constantine.*
13. *All are noted hockey broadcasters—except for Harold Ballard.*
14. *All played in the NHL for more than 20 years—except for Gainey who played for 16 years. Could be all Canadian-born except for Mikita.*
15. *All are NHL trophies for outstanding individual performance—except the Heisman, a college football award.*

Hockey Firsts

Try this multiple-choice quiz involving famous hockey "firsts."

1. The first Stanley Cup game was played in
   a. Boston b. Montreal c. Toronto d. Ottawa

2. The first U.S. team to join the NHL was
   a. New York b. Boston c. Detroit d. Chicago

3. The first defenseman to lead the NHL in scoring was
   a. Paul Coffey b. Eddie Shore c. Bobby Orr d. Doug Harvey

4. The first NHL player to score over 800 career goals was
   a. Marcel Dionne b. Rocket Richard c. Bobby Hull d. Gordie Howe

5. The first president of the NHL was a man named
   a. Campbell b. Calder c. Dutton d. Roosevelt

6. The first player to score 50 goals in a season was
   a. Gordie Howe b. Rocket Richard c. Bobby Hull d. Tiger Williams

7. The first player to score 10 points in an NHL game was
   a. Mario Lemieux b. Wayne Gretzky c. Darryl Sittler d. Frank Mahovlich

8. The first goalie to record 100 shutouts was
   a. Jacques Plante b. Johnny Bower c. Terry Sawchuk d. Frank Brimsek

9. The first player to score over 70 goals in a season was
   a. Phil Esposito b. Wayne Gretzky c. Mario Lemieux d. Bobby Hull

10. The first goaltender to win the Conn Smythe Trophy as playoff MVP was
    a. Bill Durnan b. Roger Crozier c. Ken Dryden d. Gerry Cheevers

11. In 1974, the first winner of the Jack Adams Trophy as NHL Coach of the Year was
    a. Jacques Demers b. Scotty Bowman c. Fred Shero d. Toe Blake

12. The first (and only) player to win the Conn Smythe Trophy before he won the Calder Trophy was
    a. Dave Keon b. Ken Dryden c. Serge Savard d. Wayne Gretzky

13. The first player to score 100 points in a season was
    a. Dickie Moore b. Phil Esposito c. Bobby Orr d. Darryl Sittler

14. The first coach of the New Jersey Devils was
    a. Doug Carpenter b. Jim Schoenfeld c. Billy MacMillan d. Fred Shero

15. In their first NHL season two of the following scored 51 goals. Who are they?
    a. Wayne Gretzky b. Dale Hawerchuk c. Joe Nieuwendyk d. Peter Stastny

16. He's the first defenseman to score 300 career goals. He is
    a. Bobby Orr b. Larry Robinson c. Brad Park d. Denis Potvin

17. This Flyer scored his first NHL goal on a penalty shot. He is
    a. Brian Propp b. Tim Kerr c. Ilka Sinisalo d. Rick Tocchet

18. In 1979, this player became the first member of an expansion team to win a scoring title. He is
    a. Bobby Clarke b. Bryan Trottier c. Reg Leach d. Mike Bossy

19. Two of the following share the record of eight points in a playoff game.
a. Wayne Gretzky b. Bobby Hull c. Mario Lemieux d. Patrik Sundstrom

20. The first expansion team (in 1974) to win the Stanley Cup was
a. St. Louis b. N.Y. Islanders c. Philadelphia d. Edmonton

Answers:

1. b (Montreal)	11. c (Shero)
2. b (Boston)	12. b (Dryden)
3. c (Orr)	13. b (Esposito)
4. d (Howe)	14. c (MacMillan)
5. b (Calder)	15. a&c (Gretzky and Nieuwendyk)
6. b (Richard)	16. d (Potvin)
7. c (Sittler)	17. c (Sinisalo)
8. c (Sawchuk)	18. b (Trottier)
9. a (Esposito)	19. c&d (Lemieux and Sundstrom)
10. b (Crozier)	20. c (Philadelphia)

Other Firsts . . .

When was the first penalty shot taken in the NHL?

The NHL's first penalty shot was taken on November 10, 1934, in Toronto. The shooter was Armand Mondou of the Montreal Canadiens and the goalie was little George Hainsworth, who stopped the shot. It was an important play because the Leafs won the game 2–1. Three days later Ralph (Scotty) Bowman of St. Louis became the first NHLer to score on a penalty shot when he beat goalie Alex Connell of the Montreal Maroons in St. Louis.

When and where was the first telecast of a professional hockey game?

On February 25, 1940, the New York Rangers met the Montreal Canadiens at Madison Square Garden in New York. It was the first hockey game ever televised. One camera followed the action and the event attracted only a few hundred viewers since there were only about 300 TV sets in the entire New York area.

Who was the first 16-year-old to play in the NHL?

Bep Guidolin was a lad of 16 when he joined the Boston Bruins during the 1942–43 season and was 7–15–22 in 42 games as a rookie Bruin. Guidolin got his big-league chance because at least 80 regulars in the league were serving in the armed forces.

Who was the first Soviet-trained player to play in the NHL?

During the 1982–83 season, a Soviet center named Viktor Nechayev played briefly for the L.A. Kings. Nechayev, married to an American, managed to score one goal for the Kings. When he refused demotion to the minors, the Kings released him. The second Soviet player to perform in the NHL was Sergei Priakin, who joined Calgary late in the 1988–89 season.

Goalie Jacques Plante is credited with introducing the face mask to hockey. But another goalie wore a mask briefly long before Plante's time. Who was he?

Goalie Clint Benedict, while playing for the Montreal Maroons in the twenties, stopped a Howie Morenz shot with his nose one night. Benedict asked a Boston firm to manufacture a face mask to protect his broken nose. He wore it in one game, then discarded it.

Who was the first black player to play in the NHL?

Willie O'Ree, a forward from Fredericton, N.B., became the first black player to play in the NHL during the 1957–58 season. O'Ree was signed by the Boston Bruins in January, 1958, and played in two games. He was given another opportunity in 1960–61, scored four goals in 43 games and was traded to Montreal at the end of the season.

Who was the first defenseman to score a goal?

Lester Patrick gets the credit. In 1904, the Brandon Wheat Kings were playing Winnipeg. Patrick, playing at point (defence) for Brandon, amazed onlookers when he rushed up the ice and scored a goal.

In what year were the Stanley Cup playoff games first played in three periods instead of two?

1912. The Quebec Bulldogs won the National Hockey Association championship that year and met a team from Moncton, N.B., in a playoff series, defeating the Maritimers in two straight games. Until then, games were played in two periods.

Have four players from the same team ever claimed the top four places in the individual scoring race?

Yes. In 1970–71, Phil Esposito, Bobby Orr, Johnny Bucyk and Ken Hodge comprised the top four in the individual scoring race. In 1973–74 the Bruins did it again, with Esposito, Orr, Hodge and Wayne Cashman in the first four spots.

It's in the Record Book

1. Golly Gee, you should know the name of this old timer. He shares the record with Don Murdoch, a former Ranger, for most goals in a game by a rookie (five). In 1998, he was inducted into the Hockey Hall of Fame, not as a player but as a broadcaster.

2. On December 30, 1981, Wayne Gretzky smashed a record by scoring his 50th goal in his 39th game. And he did it against Philadelphia. Who was in goal for the Flyers when he scored?
a. Pelle Lindbergh b. Wayne Stephenson c. Rick St. Croix d. nobody

3. A former Philadelphia Flyer scored his 50th goal into an empty net. He did it against Washington in 1980. That player was
a. Reg Leach b. Rick MacLeish c. Tim Kerr d. Bill Barber

4. Who holds the record for most points by a rookie?
a. Dale Hawerchuk b. Teemu Selanne
c. Mario Lemieux d. Brian Bellows

5. Which NHL team holds the record for having the most goals scored against it in one season?
a. Pittsburgh b. Washington c. Islanders d. Vancouver

6. Which NHL team holds the record for most goals scored in one season?
a. Montreal b. Philadelphia c. Edmonton d. Islanders

7. In 1928–29, the Chicago Black hawks suffered through a terrible streak. They were shut out game after game and the record they set for non-scoring is still in the books. In how many consecutive games were they shut out?
a. 5 b. 10 c. 8 d. 4

8. In that same season, the Hawks set another dubious record—fewest goals in a single season by any NHL club. How many goals did they score?
a. 99 b. 66 c. 33 d. 15

9. In 1981–82, the Pittsburgh Penguins scored a record number of power-play goals in a season—99. In 1987–88, no less than five teams broke the old Penguin record and in 1988–89 a new all-time high of 119 power-play goals was reached by
a. Calgary b. Los Angeles c. Toronto d. Pittsburgh

10. Which two defensemen were tied for most career goals (385) at the end of the 1998–99 season?
a. Bobby Orr b. Ray Bourque c. Paul Coffey d. Denis Potvin

11. As of the 1998–99 season only one NHL defenseman had compiled 1,100 career assists. He is
a. Bobby Orr b. Paul Coffey c. Ray Bourque d. Larry Robinson

12. Which NHL team holds the record for the longest unbeaten streak?
a. Montreal b. Philadelphia c. Boston d. Calgary

13. When the Montreal Canadiens scored 129 goals in 24 games in 1919–20 they didn't know they were setting a record that would last for 64 years. The record was a goals-per-game average of 5.38. In 1983–84 a new record of 5.58 goals-per-game was established by
a. Calgary b. Montreal c. Philadelphia d. Edmonton

14. When Teemu Selanne established a record for scoring by a rookie with 132 points in 1992–93, he overshadowed another rookie who collected 102 points. Selanne won the Calder Trophy that season over the runner-up who never again topped 100 points. He is
a. Joe Juneau b. Kirk Muller c. Brett Hull d. Shayne Corson

15. Which goalie holds the record for going undefeated the longest?
a. Pete Peeters b. Bernie Parent c. Turk Broda d. Gerry Cheevers

16. What is the largest margin a player has held over his nearest rival in the NHL scoring race?
a. 79 points b. 52 points c. 35 points d. 19 points

17. Who holds the single-season points record for rookie defensemen in the NHL?
    a. Denis Potvin b. Gary Suter c. Larry Murphy d. Brian Leetch

18. How many NHL players have scored 800 or more career goals?
    a. 4 b. 14 c. 24 d. 2

19. Which NHL team holds the record for the most single season 50-goal scorers on its roster? Clue: It happened in 1983–84. Was it
    a. Boston b. Montreal c. Edmonton d. Islanders

20. The most goals one team has scored in an NHL game is
    a. 20 b. 16 c. 15 d. 18

Answers:

1. *Howie Meeker, Toronto Maple Leafs.*
2. *d. Nobody. It was an empty-net goal.*
3. *a. Reg Leach.*
4. *b. Teemu Selanne, 132, with Winnipeg in 1992–93.*
5. *b. Washington, with 446 in 1974–75.*
6. *c. Edmonton. The Oilers are the only NHL team to score more than 400 goals in a season and they've done it five times. Their highest goal total was in 1983–84, when they scored 446 times.*
7. *c. They were shut out for eight straight games.*
8. *c. 33.*
9. *d. Pittsburgh.*
10. *b. Ray Bourque tied c. Paul Coffey, 385 goals as of 1998–99.*
11. *b. Paul Coffey, 1,102 assists as of 1998–99.*
12. *b. From October, 1979, through January, 1980, the Philadelphia Flyers won 25 games and tied another 10 for a record 35-game undefeated streak.*
13. *d. Edmonton.*
14. *a. Joe Juneau, Boston.*
15. *d. Gerry Cheevers of the Boston Bruins went undefeated in 32 games during the 1971–72 season. In those games, he registered 24 wins and eight ties.*
16. *a. 79 points. In 1983–84, Wayne Gretzky tallied 205 points with Edmonton. Second place went to teammate Paul Coffey with 126 points.*
17. *c. Larry Murphy still holds the record of 76 points, established in 1980–81 when he broke in with Los Angeles.*

18. *d. Two. Gordie Howe (801) and Wayne Gretzky with 894 goals as of 1998–99.*
19. *c. Edmonton. Wayne Gretzky, 87, Glenn Anderson, 54, Jari Kurri, 52.*
20. *b. 16. The record was set on March 3, 1920, at Quebec City when the Canadiens walloped the Quebec Bulldogs 16–3.*

More Fascinating Records

The NHL Guide and Record Book is filled with fascinating records. How many of them do you know?

1. Most NHL teams would be delighted to win 50 games in a season. But two NHL clubs have won as many as 60 games. Can you name them?

2. Can you name the team with the fewest wins in a season (during a minimum 70-game schedule)?

3. Can you name the NHL team holding the record for the longest undefeated streak? How long was it?

4. The longest winless streak in one NHL season is 30 games. The record belongs to the:
   a. Colorado Rockies
   b. Winnipeg Jets
   c. Kansas City Scouts

5. On March 3, 1920, playing in Quebec City, a team scored a record number of goals in a game. Name the team and the number of goals.

6. On March 19, 1981, an NHL team scored a record 9 goals in one period in a 14–4 victory over Toronto. Was the winning team:
   a. Detroit
   b. Montreal
   c. Buffalo

7. The Edmonton Oilers hold a record for having three players score 50 or more goals during the same season—and the same three players did it again two years later. Can you name the players?

8. It's hard to imagine a goaltender going six games in a row without allowing a goal. But that's the NHL record for most consecutive shutouts held by:
   a. Georges Vezina
   b. George Hainsworth
   c. George Plimpton
   d. Alex Connell

9. It's difficult to believe but a team once scored a puny total of 33 goals in one season. Was this impotent group the:
   a. Washington Capitals
   b. Ottawa Senators
   c. Chicago Blackhawks

10. The record for the fewest goals in one season during a minimum 70-game schedule is held by the:
    a. Washington Capitals
    b. Ottawa Senators
    c. Chicago Blackhawks

11. Only one NHL player has averaged over 2 points per game in his NHL career, which ended in 1997 after 12 seasons. Can you name him?

12. In 1996–97 a rookie Penguin made a sensational debut in goal, establishing a record for the longest undefeated streak by a goalie from the start of his career—14 wins and 2 ties. A year later he was back in the minors. Can you name him?

13. Wayne Gretzky scored 60 or more goals in a season five times in 20 years. But another scoring star shares the record with Gretzky, with five 60-goal seasons in just 10 seasons. Who is he?

14. Teemu Selanne holds the NHL record for most goals by a rookie in one season—76. Who holds the record for most points by a rookie in a season?

15. Here's one that isn't in the *NHL Guide* because it's not the kind of record that gets published. Name the player who tied a record by playing with four NHL clubs during the 1998–99 season. Who was it?

a. Jocelyn Thibeault
b. Dave Manson
c. Roman Vopat

Answers:

1. *Detroit (62 games in 1995–96) and Montreal (60 games in 1976–77).*
2. *Washington (with 8 in 1974–75).*
3. *Philadelphia (35 games before losing to Minnesota in 1979–1980).*
4. *b. Winnipeg Jets. The Jets were winless in 30 during the 1980–81 season.*
5. *Montreal Canadiens. The Habs beat the Quebec Bulldogs 16–3.*
6. *c. Buffalo.*
7. *In 1983–84, Wayne Gretzky scored 87, Glenn Anderson scored 54 and Jari Kurri scored 52. In 1985–86, Kurri scored 68, Anderson scored 54 and Gretzky scored 52.*
8. *d. Alex Connell, Ottawa Senators, 1927–28.*
9. *c. Chicago Blackhawks in 1928–29 during a 44-game schedule.*
10. *c. Chicago Blackhawks, 133 goals in 1953–54 in 70 games.*
11. *Mario Lemieux (2.01 points per game).*
12. *Patrick Lalime.*
13. *Mike Bossy.*
14. *Selanne (132 in 1992–93).*
15. *c. Roman Vopat. Center "Suitcase" Vopat started the season with Los Angeles, was traded to Colorado, who traded him to Chicago, who traded him to Philadelphia—all in the span of a month. The only other NHLer to play with four clubs in one season (1977–78) was Dennis O'Brien, a defenseman.*

Birthplaces

Can you match these current and former NHL players with their birthplaces?

1.	Patrick Roy	a.	Chicago, Illinois
2.	The Sutters	b.	New York City
3.	Wayne Gretzky	c.	Bratislava, Czechoslovakia
4.	Gordie Howe	d.	Warroad, Minnesota
5.	Peter Stastny	e.	Thurso, Quebec
6.	Joey Mullen	f.	Floral, Saskatchewan
7.	Chris Chelios	g.	Parry Sound, Ontario
8.	Jari Kurri	h.	Viking, Alberta

9.	Mats Naslund	i.	Montreal, Quebec
10.	Guy Lafleur	j.	Brantford, Ontario
11.	Bobby Orr	k.	Quebec City
12.	Mario Lemieux	l.	Timra, Sweden
13.	Dave Christian	m.	Helsinki, Finland
14.	Brian Leetch	n.	Medicine Hat, Alberta
15.	Trevor Linden	o.	Corpus Christi, Texas
16.	Jeremy Roenick	p.	Vancouver, B.C.
17.	Dominik Hasek	q.	Moscow, USSR
18.	Paul Kariya	r.	Pardubice, Czechoslovakia
19.	Sergei Samsonov	s.	Boston
20.	Brian Dafoe	t.	Sussex, England

Answers:
1. -k, 2. -h, 3. -j, 4. -f, 5. -c, 6. -b, 7. -a, 8. -m, 9. -l, 10. -e, 11. -g, 12. -i, 13. -d, 14. -o, 15. -n, 16. -s, 17. -r, 18. -p, 19. -q, 20. -t.

Did You Know?

How is the ice surface made in a modern-day arena?

In most big-league arenas the ice surface is kept at a temperature of 11°F. The ice is approximately three-quarters of an inch thick. A brine solution is circulated through several miles of pipe buried beneath the concrete floor of the arena. This coolant flowing through the pipes chills the floor surface above. When water is applied to the floor, along with a substance that gives the ice its white color, the liquid quickly freezes. The lines are painted on by hand, as are any team logos. The lines and designs are "pebbled" with a light spray of water to seal the paint and make the ice ready for play.

What does the Zamboni do?

The Zamboni ice-making machine circles the arena at hockey games after the pre-game warmup and between periods. The machine simply takes off a layer of ice and lays another one down. The machine lowers a scraper that shaves off a thin layer of ice and snow. This is dumped, by means of a conveyor belt, into a large bin on top of the Zamboni. Meanwhile, a light coating of hot water is being applied to the ice surface from the back of the machine. In five or ten minutes, the water has frozen to a clean, smooth surface.

What is Jet Ice?

Jet Ice, developed by the late Doug Moore, chief engineer at Maple Leaf Gardens for 30 years, is an ice-making technique that has revolutionized the ice-making industry. All the impurities and minerals are removed from the water laid down by the Zamboni. This results in harder, faster ice, energy savings and lower maintenance costs. Many NHL arenas are now using the Jet Ice system.

Which city built the first indoor artificial ice rink?

In 1842, Henry Kirk, an Englishman, invented a form of artificial ice using alum, grease and ammonia. By 1865, other inventors were making huge slabs of much harder ice using a refrigerant of brine and carbonic acid. A few years later, in 1876, London sportsman John Gangee built a tiny arena called the Glacarium for his personal use. It measured 24 by 40 feet. A year later, a large arena opened for skating in Manchester. Before the turn of the century there were artificial ice rinks operating in Manchester, London, Paris, New York and Pittsburgh. The first arena in the U.S., covering 6,000 square feet, was opened in Madison Square Garden in 1879.

Hockey researcher Pete Wevurski claims that Pittsburgh became the site of the first indoor rink with artificial ice for hockey in 1894 when the Casino opened in a place called Schenley Park. When the Casino burned down two years later, another arena was constructed and a four-team hockey league, with players imported from Canada, made use of the new Duquesne Garden, which opened in 1899. New York historians claim hockey was played on the St. Nicholas arena when it opened in 1897.

When was artificial ice introduced to Canada?

Hockey in Canada was played on natural ice until 1911 when the Patrick brothers, Lester and Frank, decided to erect two arenas in British Columbia. Both housed artificial ice plants. The arena in Vancouver had over 10,000 seats, the one in Victoria was about half that size. At the time there were only 11 artificial ice rinks in the world. When the NHL began play in 1917, Toronto was the only city in the league with artificial ice.

When was artificial ice introduced in Russia?

Not until the late forties. By 1950, Soviet hockey players were able to skate on artificial ice for the first time. The ice surface was tiny and there was room for only one goal net but it was a beginning. In a few years, Soviet teams were winning world championships.

How does the NHL define a shot on goal?

In the NHL, a shot on goal means any deliberate action taken by an attacking player to shoot or deflect the puck with his stick into the opposing goal and which actually enters the net or which, except by the intervention of the goalie or any other players, would have entered the goal. This does not include shots that hit the goal post or do not go in the net.

If a goalie is on his way to a shutout, then gets hurt and is replaced in goal, who gets credit for the resulting shutout?

When a team records a shutout and more than one goaltender plays for that team, none of the goaltenders receives credit for the shutout but the team is credited with one.

If a player dresses for a game but does not get into the game, is he credited with a "game played" in the league stats?

No. A player is not credited with a "game played" in the NHL unless he actually gets on the ice and plays.

Doubleheaders (two games in one day) used to be a big part of baseball. Has the NHL ever scheduled doubleheaders?

No, with one exception. In 1937, at a new rink in Saskatoon, Saskatchewan, the New York Rangers and the New York Americans agreed to play a doubleheader while preparing for the new season. There was such a demand to see the one game scheduled that it was decided to play a second. The referee for both games was Clarence Campbell, who went on to become NHL president.

Why does no Pittsburgh player wear sweater No. 21?

Sweater No. 21 belonged to Penguin rookie Michel Briere, who played one season for the club in 1968–69. This brilliant young player was critically injured in an auto accident after his initial season and remained in a coma for almost a year before passing away on May 13, 1971. His sweater has been retired by the Penguins and remains on display in the team's Igloo Club.

Who were the Baby Bulls and where did they play?

In 1978, the Birmingham Bulls of the WHA made a bold move. They signed five teenagers from junior hockey in Canada at a time when NHL clubs wrestled with the problem of accepting players under the age of 20. Player agents Alan Eagleson and Bill Watters approached Bulls' owner John Bassett, Jr., with a package deal, one he immediately accepted. He would get defenseman Craig Hartsburg, Rob Ramage and Gaston Gingras, goalie Pat Riggin and forward Rick Vaive and Michel Goulet, each one a standout in junior hockey. The sextet became known as the Baby Bulls. Another teenager already signed by Birmingham was forward Ken Linseman.

Which team has shown the most dramatic improvement from one season to the next?

In 1981–82, the Winnipeg Jets showed a startling 48-point improvement over their point total from the previous season. They went from nine wins and 32 points in 1980–81 to 33 wins and 80 points the next season. Jets' coach Tom Watt earned Coach-of-the-Year honors for engineering the most dynamic turnaround in league history. Nevertheless, a few months later, he was fired.

Name the player who fashioned the most dramatic single-season improvement in NHL history as reflected in his scoring points. His accomplishment came during the 1988–89 season.

In 1988–89, Bernie Nicholls of the Los Angeles Kings collected 70 goals and 80 assists for 150 points. The previous season he had scored 78 points (32 goals and 46 assists). That represents an improvement of 72 points, the greatest single-season increase since the NHL began play in 1917. Only players who played at least 80 per cent of their teams' games in consecutive seasons were included in the survey. The previous high was 63 points, recorded by Guy Lafleur of the Canadiens who went from 56 points in 1973–74 to 119 points the following season.

Have there been many incidents of drug abuse by players in the NHL?

A few. There was the March, 1989, arrest of Detroit Red Wings player Bob Probert, who was charged with smuggling 14.3 grams of cocaine into the U.S. Prior to that, in 1983, Ric Nattress, then with Montreal, pleaded guilty to possessing a small amount of hashish and marijuana. He received a year's suspension from the NHL, although the penalty was later commuted to 30 days. In 1978, Ranger star Don Murdoch was caught with 4.5 grams of cocaine in his luggage at Toronto's Pearson International Airport. He pleaded guilty, received a suspended sentence, and was suspended for one year by the NHL. His suspension was later reduced to 40 games. In 1986, Borje Salming of the Leafs admitted to experimenting with cocaine several years earlier. He was suspended for eight games and fined $500. Former NHLer Steve Durbano was arrested in 1981 and charged with attempting to bring cocaine into Canada. In 1983, he was sentenced to seven years and served 28 months. Durbano said, "When I played for Pittsburgh in 1974 there seemed to be cocaine everywhere."

Years ago, why was the NHL often referred to as "the Norris House League"?

The late James Norris and his family once owned the Detroit Olympia and the Red Wings, Chicago Stadium, and a controlling interest in Madison Square Garden. With half the NHL's six teams playing in these arenas, it's easy to understand the "Norris House League" appellation.

What was the "Curse of Muldoon"?

It was a story conceived in the fertile imagination of sportswriter Jim Coleman. When Pete Muldoon, the first of a number of coaches to be fired in Chicago, was dismissed, Coleman told his readers Muldoon had placed a curse on the Hawks, a hex that would keep them from ever finishing in first place in the NHL. Strangely, Muldoon was fired in 1927 and it was 40 years before the Hawks found themselves atop the league standings.

Who was the youngest referee ever to handle a Stanley Cup game?

Ages of early-day referees in Stanley Cup play were seldom recorded but Frank Patrick would certainly rank among the youngest. Frank was not only a star player but he refereed in the Montreal Senior League at age 18 and handled a Stanley Cup game at age 20.

Why don't referees help linesmen break up fights?

The referee stands back when a fight breaks out. It is his

responsibility to take note of what is happening, who caused the fight and what penalties might be meted out as a result.

Has the NHL ever placed a ceiling on players' salaries?

Yes. In 1932, the league owners decided that no player should earn more than $7,500 in one season. After two seasons, when the players didn't complain about the salary cap, the owners lowered the maximum salary to $7,000.

Has a pro player ever been reprimanded for rough play by his own coach or manager?

Yes. When Sprague Cleghorn was traded from Ottawa to Montreal in 1921 he appeared to have sworn a vendetta against his former mates. In one game in the 1923 playoffs he assaulted Ottawa's Lionel Hitchman with a vicious cross-check. As a result, he drew a match penalty and, from his own manager Leo Dandurand, a fine of $200 and a suspension from the final game. Dandurand also banned a second player, Billy Coutu, from the final game after Coutu clubbed an Ottawa player to the ice in the opening game of the series.

Who is the only player known to have played all positions during a Stanley Cup playoff?

Ottawa's versatile Frank (King) Clancy, in the 1923 Stanley Cup playoffs in Vancouver played all three forward and both defensive positions in a game against Edmonton. During the game, he even got a chance to play goal. Ottawa goalie Clint Benedict was given a two-minute penalty. In those days the goaltender served his time like the other players. Benedict tossed his stick to Clancy, saying, "Take care of that net 'til I get back." Clancy was not scored on and Ottawa went on to win the series and the Stanley Cup.

Did a player once win the NHL scoring title while compiling only four assists?

Yes. In 1926–27, Bill Cook of the New York Rangers edged Dick Irvin of Chicago by one point in the NHL scoring race. Cook scored 33 goals and 4 assists for 37 points that season. Irvin had 18 goals and 18 assists for 36 points.

Who is the oldest player to register a 50-goal season in the NHL?

In the 69th game of the 1970–71 season, on March 16, 1971, Johnny Bucyk became the oldest player to score 50 goals in a season. He collected goals number 49 and 50 when Boston whipped Detroit 11–4. At the time Bucyk was 35 years old.

The WHA lured some big names away from the NHL, including Bobby Hull, Marc Tardif, Frank Mahovlich and Derek Sanderson. Who was the WHA's all-time leading scorer with 798 points?

Andre Lacroix.

How many players is a team allowed to carry on its roster?

Teams in the NHL are allowed to carry as many players as they wish on their rosters, but a team may dress only 18 skaters and two goaltenders for each game.

How is the trading deadline decided each year?

The trading deadline is always the 26th day preceding the end of the regular season.

Has a player ever had his name engraved on the Stanley Cup without having played for the winning team?

Yes. The 1929 Cup champion Boston Bruins insisted that goaltender Hal Winkler's name be engraved on the Cup—even though Winkler had retired after the 1927–28 season and didn't play a single game for the Bruins during their run to the Cup. The Bruins wanted to show their appreciation for his fine play during the previous season. The Detroit Red Wings also had injured player Vladimir Konstantinov's name engraved on the cup in 1998, even though his final game was in 1997.

Have the greatest moments in NHL history ever been listed?

In 1996, Mastercard polled 400 writers and broadcasters and announced three finalists in their search for the NHL's Greatest Moments. The finalists were named The New York Rangers ending their 54-year drought by winning the 1994 Stanley Cup; the Montreal Canadiens record fifth consecutive Cup victory in 1960 and Bobby Orr's acrobatic overtime goal that won the Cup for Boston in 1970. Orr's goal was later named the Greatest Moment, even though it ended a less than thrilling four-game sweep of the St. Louis Blues

Because of their love for hockey, some players have said they'd play in the NHL for nothing. Has it ever happened?

No, but a player once signed a contract for a dollar a year. In 1930, a 26-year-old defenseman named Charlie "Dinny" Dinsmore, a player who'd retired from the Montreal Maroons two years earlier to become a bond salesman, decided to make a comeback. He agreed to play for a dollar. He played in nine games for an average stipend of a little more than ten cents per game, only to be released at the end of the season.

Have two teams ever become involved in a brawl before the start of a game?

Yes. In the spring of 1987, before the start of the sixth playoff game in a series between Montreal and Philadelphia, a major brawl broke out—all because of a silly superstition.

It was triggered by the Habs' habit of shooting the puck—for good luck—into the opposing team's empty net at the end of the warmup. When Shayne Corson and Claude Lemieux slipped the puck into the net, the Flyers' Ed Hospodar, en route to the dressing room, became incensed. He jumped back on the ice and attacked Lemieux. Players from both teams leaped over the boards and began brawling.

The teams were fined more than $24,000 each and Hospodar was suspended for the balance of the playoffs.

What's the strangest coaching strategy ever concocted?

The honors go to a man named Godfrey Matheson, one of three coaches employed by the Chicago Blackhawks in 1932–33. Matheson's weirdest innovation was the whistle system of coaching. From the bench he blew a whistle to direct his players on the ice. One blast was a signal for the puck carrier to pass the puck, two blasts called for a shot on goal, three blasts meant to start back-checking and so on. One can only imagine how the referee reacted to all the whistle-blowing. Major McLaughlin, the team owner, wasn't thrilled with Matheson's antics, either. He fired him after just two games.

Has a player agent ever been convicted of stealing money from his clients?

In the mid-seventies, player agent Dick Sorkin of Long Island was one of the most successful men in his field with big name clients like Bob Nystrom, Tom Lysiak and Lanny McDonald. The young men he represented had complete confidence in Sorkin and allowed him to handle all their finances. They didn't know he was taking their money and investing it in the stock market. When the market collapsed, Sorkin's losses were staggering. He tried to make up for them by taking more money and gambling it on sporting events. Finally, when the players demanded an accounting, he admitted the money was gone. He was charged with fraud, found guilty and sentenced to three years in jail.

Great Goalies

Who was the greatest goalie in U.S. college history?

My vote goes to Ken Dryden who starred at Cornell before helping the Montreal Canadiens win six Stanley Cups. A look at Dryden's college stats reveals a mark of 76–4–1 in three years of varsity play. His save percentage was .939, his goals-against average was 1.59 and he recorded 13 shutouts.

As one of hockey's all-time greats, did goalie Terry Sawchuk have one memorable playoff series?

Sawchuk had several, but one does stand out. In 1952, he played four games on home ice in Detroit and didn't give up a goal. In the opening playoff round, Sawchuk and the Wings beat Toronto 3–0 and 1–0 at home. They eliminated Toronto with two straight wins at Maple Leaf Gardens, with Sawchuk giving up three goals in the two games. Then, because of a booking conflict, the final series with Montreal opened at the Forum in Montreal. Sawchuk gave up just two goals as the Wings beat the Habs 3–1 and 2–1. Back in Detroit, Sawchuk chalked up back-to-back shutouts, both by 3–0 scores. In two series, against strong opposition, he'd given up a mere five goals. Sawchuk's four shutouts in an eight-game sweep by the Wings was an incredible feat.

Among NHL goaltenders, who would be rated the top playoff performers?

Old-timers will tell you that Turk Broda of the Leafs (who once surrendered only 34 goals in a span of 24 playoff games), Terry Sawchuk of Detroit (who allowed just five goals in eight games in the 1952 playoffs and chalked up four shutouts), Jacques Plante of Montreal (who had an extraordinary 1.90 average when the Habs won five consecutive Stanley Cups in the late fifties) and Alex Connell of Ottawa, Detroit and the Montreal Maroons (who played on two Cup winners and owned a 1.19 average in 21 playoff games) were arguably the best under playoff pressure.

In the modern era, Ken Dryden of Montreal often played brilliantly in leading the Habs to six Cups in nine years; Billy Smith of the Islanders was a key figure in the Islanders' romp to four Stanley Cups and Bernie Parent led the Flyers to back-to-back Cups in 1974 and '75. He won the Conn Smythe Trophy both years. A big-league coach would feel confident having any one of the above as his goalie at playoff time. Others who have shone in the Cup playoffs include Grant Fuhr, Johnny Bower, Glenn Hall, Bill Durnan, Roger Crozier, Gerry Cheevers, Patrick Roy, Mike Vernon and Dominik Hasek.

In the past 50 years, has any NHL goalie recorded as many as 15 shutouts in a season?

Yes. Tony Esposito of Chicago chalked up 15 shutouts during the 1969–70 season.

Which goalie holds the record for most shots faced in a game?

On March 4, 1941, goalie Sam LoPresti faced 83 Boston Bruin shots while tending goal for Chicago. It's an all-time record. Amazingly, the Bruins beat Chicago by the slimmest of margins, 3–2.

Why was goalie Gary Smith called "Suitcase" Smith?

Smith earned the nickname "Suitcase" because he seldom had time to unpack it. In a pro career that covered 15 seasons, Smith played for seven different NHL teams, plus five other teams in the minor leagues and Indianapolis in the WHA.

Frankie Brimsek, a native of Virginia, Minnesota, was absolutely brilliant when he became Boston's No. 1 goaltender in 1938. Has any other netminder ever matched his first few NHL starts?

No. Early in the 1938–39 season, rookie Brimsek replaced Boston's regular netminder Tiny Thompson on two occasions and won both his starts. Then he was sent back to the American League. In December, 1938, when Thompson was sold to Detroit, Brimsek was recalled and became the Bruins' starting goalie. He made a smashing debut, putting together a string of three straight shutouts and six in seven games. It's a mark that may never be matched. When the season was over, he'd captured the Vezina Trophy, the Calder Trophy, and was the first rookie in history to make the first All-Star team.

Who was the youngest goalie ever to play in the NHL?

World War II was at its peak when 17-year-old Harry Lumley of Owen Sound, Ontario, became the youngest goalie to perform in the NHL. Harry played two games for the Detroit Red Wings that season and put together a 6.50 goals-against average. Lumley is the only goalie ever to play for two NHL teams in his first 24 hours in the league. After making his debut for Detroit, the following night he was recruited by the Rangers to replace regular netminder Ken McAuley, who was injured. The next year Lumley became a regular, playing in 37 games and compiling a 3.22 average. Harry was slightly older when he broke in than 16-year-old forward Bep Guidolin of Boston, the youngest player in league history.

Has a goalie ever been captain of an NHL team?

Bill Durnan of Montreal was one of the last goalie captains in the NHL. Durnan played for the Canadiens from 1943 to 1950.

When did goalies begin wearing pads on their legs?

Even before the turn of the century goalies were protecting their shins with flimsy pads. In 1896, the Winnipeg Vics took the ice in Ottawa for a Stanley Cup game and Merritt, the Vics' goalie, was wearing white cricket pads. Despite protests that the pads were illegal, Merritt insisted on wearing them and he recorded a shutout in the game, the first in Cup history.

The two Dryden brothers faced each other during the 1970–71 season. Was this a first for NHL goalies?

Yes. On March 20, 1971, at the Montreal Forum, two goaltending brothers, Ken Dryden of Montreal and Dave Dryden of Buffalo, played against each other in an NHL game. It almost didn't happen, even though Buffalo coach Punch Imlach tried his utmost to ensure that it would. Imlach started Dave Dryden in goal, hoping the Canadiens would start

Ken and create history. But coach Al MacNeil chose Rogatien Vachon as Montreal's starting goalie. Imlach then withdrew his Dryden and replaced him with Joe Daley. Coincidence caused the match-up. Vachon was injured in the second period and Ken Dryden replaced him. Imlach immediately yanked Daley and Dave Dryden took over. Montreal won 5–2, and after the game the two brothers skated to center ice, where they shook hands and received a tremendous ovation from the fans.

When did goalie Glenn Hall's iron-man streak for consecutive games come to an end?

Hall's amazing "iron-man" record was brought to an end in November, 1962, when he left the nets suffering from a strained back. He had participated in 502 consecutive games (551 counting the playoffs), before Denis DeJordy took over. Hall recovered to win the Vezina Trophy that season.

Goaltender Quiz

Rookie level

1. He won back-to-back Conn Smythe Trophies for Philadelphia in 1974 and 1975.

2. He captured the Vezina Trophy four times in the nineties.

3. He backstopped Montreal to Stanley Cups in 1986 and 1993.

4. He starred in goal for the Red Wings when they captured the Cup in 1997.

5. He was the victim of Paul Henderson's famous goal in 1972.

Major League level

6. He was in goal for Boston the night Darryl Sittler set a record with 10 points in a game.

7. He played a record number of minutes (57,228) in his career.

8. In 1973–74, he set a record by winning 47 games.

9. He helped the Islanders win four Stanley Cups from 1980 to 1983, winning 57 playoff games.

10. He was the opposing goaltender when Bobby Orr scored the Stanley Cup–winning goal in overtime in 1970.

All-Star level

11. He became the first goaltender in history to jump directly from U.S. high school hockey to the NHL.

12. He was the last goaltender to win the Calder Trophy (in 1994).

13. A Minnesota native, in 1938–39 he won 11 of his first 15 games as a rookie including six by shutouts.

14. He holds the NHL record for consecutive shutouts with six.

15. This Chicago goalie once stopped a record 80 shots in a game. His son also played goal in the NHL for six seasons.

Answers:
1. Bernie Parent, 2. Dominik Hasek, 3. Patrick Roy, 4. Mike Vernon, 5. Vladislav Tretiak, 6. Dave Reece, 7. Terry Sawchuk, 8. Bernie Parent, 9. Billy Smith, 10. Glenn Hall, 11. Tom Barrasso, 12. Martin Brodeur, 13. Frank Brimsek, 14. Alex Connell, 15. Sam LoPresti, father of Pete.

Great Lines

1. Ab McDonald was a member of Chicago's Scooter Line. Who were the other two players on the line?

2. Chicago had another line called the Million Dollar Line. Who played on it?

3. Who were the members of the Production Line?

Gordie Howe played 32 demanding seasons in five different decades and established more records than any other player.

4. In the seventies, New York's GAG Line was hot. Can you name the line members? What did the initials GAG stand for?

5. One of Boston's first great lines was the Kraut Line. Who were the members?

6. In the fifties, another good line for Boston was called the Uke Line. Do you remember who played on it?

7. Rocket Richard was the most famous member of Montreal's Punch Line. But the other two members could score, too. Who were they?

8. Shortly after Maple Leaf Gardens opened, members of the Kid Line became national idols. Who were they?

9. Name the members of Legion of Doom Line from 1995–97.

10. Name the line Dionne, Simmer and Taylor played on with the Kings.

11. Name the three players on Buffalo's potent French Connection Line.

12. When Phil Esposito scored 76 goals in 1970–71, he credited two linemates for helping him to the record total. Who were they?

Answers:

1. *Stan Mikita and Kenny Wharram*
2. *Bobby Hull, Bill Hay and Murray Balfour*
3. *Ted Lindsay, Gordie Howe and Sid Abel*
4. *Rod Gilbert, Vic Hadfield and Jean Ratelle made up the GAG Line. GAG stood for goal-a-game.*
5. *Milt Schmidt, Bobby Bauer and Porky Dumart*
6. *Bronco Horvath, Vic Stasiuk and Johnny Bucyk*
7. *Elmer Lach and Toe Blake*
8. *Charlie Conacher, Busher Jackson and Joe Primeau*
9. *John LeClair, Eric Lindros and Mikael Renberg*
10. *The Triple Crown Line*
11. *Rene Robert, Gilbert Perreault and Richard Martin*
12. *Wayne Cashman and Ken Hodge*

Would You Believe It?

Did it happen in hockey or didn't it? Many bizarre events have occurred in the game over the years. Some of the following are fiction, some are fact. You decide which stories are true and which are false.

1. A famous Toronto player once played in a game at Maple Leaf Gardens wearing a green uniform instead of the traditional blue and white Leaf colors.

2. In the middle of a Stanley Cup game, a referee became angry with the players, announced he was through for the night, took off his skates and went home.

3. In the long history of the NHL, only once has a Stanley Cup winner not been declared.

4. One old-time player performed in only 23 regular season games in his entire career and still scored 63 goals in Stanley Cup playoff games.

5. The Boston Bruins allowed a sportswriter to play in goal for them once even though he'd never played the position before.

6. When a player was asked to give the puck to the referee in an NHL game, he refused. The referee skated off and awarded the game to the opposing team.

7. A goaltender in the NHL once registered six straight shutouts.

8. An NHL team once played eight consecutive games without scoring a goal.

9. A professional coach once called a meeting of the players' wives and asked them to stop having sex with their husbands for the good of the team.

10. Four sets of brothers once played in the same NHL game.

11. Lord Stanley, Canada's first Prime Minister, donated the Stanley Cup in 1893.

12. Some early-day goalies spit tobacco juice down the open end of the hollow goal posts in use at that time.

13. One hockey star in the early years of the NHL was kidnapped by gamblers, but managed to knock out his captors with a hockey stick. Then he rushed to the Montreal Forum in time to score the winning goal in a playoff game.

14. A hockey Hall-of-Famer didn't learn how to skate until he was in his mid-teens. Until then he played hockey in his street shoes.

15. A sportswriter was once hired as a back-up goalie for a big-league team.

16. Eddie Johnston was the last goaltender to appear in all of his team's regular-season games. He played for Boston in all 70 games in 1963–64.

17. A big-league goalie, miffed that the starting assignment he anticipated was given to a rookie just up from the minors, waited until the national anthem was played, then skated to the dressing room, took off his uniform, and went home.

18. Kate Smith once refereed a game at the Spectrum in Philadelphia.

19. A fan once broke a glass showcase in the Chicago Stadium housing the Stanley Cup, scooped up the gleaming trophy and tried to run off with it.

20. An NHL player scored his first big-league goal when Harry Truman was president of the U.S. and his last when Ronald Reagan was in the White House.

Answers:

1. *True. King Clancy wore a green uniform for the Leafs on King Clancy Night at the Gardens, March 17, 1934. His green jersey had a big shamrock pinned to the back.*

2. True. In 1899, during a Stanley Cup game between Winnipeg and Montreal, referee Findlay became angry with the players when they refused to accept one of his decisions. So he took off his skates and went home. Officials chased after him in a sleigh and persuaded him to come back but Winnipeg refused to return to the ice. The game was awarded to Montreal.

3. True. In 1919, the sixth game of the Stanley Cup series between Montreal and Seattle was canceled when the flu epidemic decimated the ranks of the teams involved. The series was never finished and Bad Joe Hall, one of hockey's toughest players, died of the flu a few days later. It's the only time in NHL history a final series has not been completed.

4. True. Frank McGee did it. Incredible as it seems, McGee played in a mere 23 regular season games with Ottawa from 1903 to 1906, scoring 71 goals. In Stanley Cup play, he was almost as phenomenal, scoring 63 goals in 22 games.

5. True. On October 6, 1976, writer George Plimpton played in goal for the Bruins during an exhibition game with the Philadelphia Flyers. Even though he'd had no previous goaltending experience, he stopped a Reg Leach penalty shot during his brief stint in nets.

6. True. On February 27, 1926, Toronto's Babe Dye refused to give the puck to referee Bobby Hewitson after a fight on the ice. So Hewitson awarded the game to Montreal and skated off.

7. True. During the 1927–28 season, goalie Alex Connell of Ottawa played six consecutive games without allowing a single goal.

8. True. In 1928–29, the Chicago Black hawks set a record for futility that may last forever. They played in eight straight games without scoring a single goal. In fact, during the 44-game schedule, the Hawks were shut out 20 times and scored a team total of 33 goals for the entire season.

9. True. According to Don Cherry, who was there when it happened, Springfield owner-coach Eddie Shore called a meeting of his players and their wives. He told the wives the team was going badly because they were having too much sex with their husbands.

10. True. On December 1, 1940, there were four sets of brothers on the ice for a game between New York and Chicago. Lynn and Muzz Patrick and Neil and Mac Colville played for the Rangers while Bob and Bill Carse and Max and Doug Bentley played for the Hawks.

11. False. Lord Stanley donated the Cup that year but he wasn't Canada's prime minister. He was governor general at the time.

12. True. In early years the goal had no crossbar. The posts were hollow and uncapped at the top, a perfect repository or makeshift spittoon for tobacco-chewing goalies like Bert Lindsay.

Henri Richard, younger brother of Maurice, won a record 11
Stanley Cups while playing for the Canadiens.

13. **False.**

14. **True.** *Georges Vezina was the Hall-of-Famer who didn't learn how to skate until his teens. He preferred to play in goal in his street shoes.*

15. **True.** *In the fifties, when teams carried but one goalie on the roster, backup goalies of questionable competence were called on in the event of an injury. These netminders were supplied by the home team. The Montreal Canadiens, during the 1959–60 season, figured that one of the hockey writers on the beat was a better bet than that. So they signed Jacques Beauchamp to a contract. Alas, much as he hungered for it, Beauchamp never got a chance to show his stuff.*

16. **True.**

17. **True.** *Al Smith was the goalie. It happened in Buffalo when Punch Imlach decided to call up Don Edwards and give him a start.*

18. **False, but she was the Flyers' most famous anthem singer.**

19. **True.** *A Montreal fan, Ken Killander, watching his beloved Canadiens lose to Chicago in a 1962 playoff game, smashed the showcase, grabbed the Cup and ran. Arrested and brought to court, he told the judge he was "merely taking it back to Montreal where it belongs." The judge sent him back to Montreal.*

20. **True.** *Gordie Howe broke in during the Truman administration and bowed out when Reagan was newly elected.*

Hockey Oddities

What NHL team attempted to change players' names to attract more ethnic fans?

When the New York Rangers joined the NHL, publicity men for the club attempted to persuade goalie Lorne Chabot to change his name to Chabotsky to attract Jewish fans. Another Ranger, Oliver Reinikka, was to be given the name Rocco to please Italian supporters. There was even a plan to have two fake gunmen kidnap Ranger star Bill Cook to drum up publicity for the team.

Did an NHL player change his name to accommodate the newsmen who covered his team?

Yes. Steve Wojciechowski changed his name to Steve Wochy when he played for Detroit in 1944–45.

How many games did the old Brooklyn Americans play in Brooklyn?

The Brooklyn Americans didn't play any of their games in Brooklyn. They played home games in Madison Square Garden, the home of the Rangers. The New York Americans changed their name to Brooklyn Americans in the 1941–42 season. It was an effort to take advantage of the popularity of the Brooklyn Dodgers baseball team.

Which NHL goalie dashed up the ice and almost scored a goal 40 years before Ron Hextall of the Flyers made history?

In 1946, long before the rule existed prohibiting goaltenders from skating past center ice, Charlie Rayner of the New York Rangers almost scored a goal against Harry Lumley of the Red Wings. When referee King Clancy called two penalties within seconds of each other against Detroit, Rayner stopped a shot, then lumbered up the ice. He passed to a teammate at the Wings' blueline and kept going, right into the high slot area in front of opposing goalie Harry Lumley. Neil Colville whipped a pass to Rayner and he drilled a shot off the goal post.

What hockey record did Bill Mosienko set that made him famous?

In 1952, in the final game of the season, the Chicago Black hawks faced the New York Rangers. In goal for New York was rookie Lorne Anderson. Chicago forward Bill Mosienko beat Anderson for three goals in a mere 21 seconds, with Gus Bodnar assisting on all three. It's a record that stands to this day. Anderson never played another NHL game while Mosienko scored 258 career goals and became a member of the Hockey Hall of Fame.

Name the only NHL player who scored a goal while playing with a broken back.

During a game in Chicago in 1964–65, Dean Prentice of the Bruins was hauled down on a breakaway by Stan Mikita. Prentice was injured on the play, and was unaware he'd been awarded a penalty shot until he was helped to his feet by teammates. Still groggy, he elected to take the shot. He beat goalie Denis Dejordy with the free shot, then went to the hospital where x-rays revealed a fractured vertebra.

Who was the player who paid his fine in pennies?

Many years ago, Ken Randall of Toronto owed the league a total of $35 in fines. On the eve of a game with Ottawa, Randall was told to pay the fine before the opening face-off or be suspended. Randall begged here and borrowed there and by game time he found he had just enough money to pay the fine—$32 in bills and $3 in pennies. League officials accepted the bills but refused to take the pennies. Randall, peeved at this decision, threw the bag of pennies on the ice where they rolled in all directions. The referee refused to start the game until the coins were collected. Randall and his teammates spent the next few minutes scooping up the pennies. Randall somehow converted them to bills, paid his fine and took his place in the starting lineup.

Where did the idea of selecting three stars of a game originate?

In the thirties, Foster Hewitt began selecting three stars after Leaf games as a tie-in with a three-star brand of gasoline, one of the sponsors of his broadcasts. In those days, a player chosen as a game star received a small silver spoon as a souvenir of the occasion.

Which NHL scoring champ once invaded a rival team's arena and claimed it as a Canadian colony?

Gordon Drillon, the last Leaf player to win a scoring title back in 1938. In retirement, he never lost his zest for the game. In the mid-sixties, Drillon led a wild band of Maritimers onto the ice at the Boston Garden one night, raised the Canadian flag, and claimed the Garden as a colony for Saint John, New Brunswick. One Boston fan commented, "Anybody crazy enough to claim this old barn should be forced to take it."

What player was vilified by his own team's fans for winning a scoring title?

Boom Boom Geoffrion of Montreal. Geoffrion is surely the only player to be vilified by his hometown supporters for winning the league scoring crown in 1954–55. That was the year Rocket Richard, en route to the scoring title, was suspended after a stick-swinging battle with Boston's Hal Laycoe. Richard was suspended for the rest of the season and the playoffs, a penalty that triggered the famous St. Patrick's Day riot in Montreal and cost Richard his only chance at a scoring title. When Geoffrion won it, he was booed.

Talk about hungry hockey players. What player who retired in 1923 established a reputation as hockey's biggest eater?

When Harry Mummery, at 258 pounds, joined the Montreal Canadiens in 1916 he handed the manager a food bill for $107, which covered his dining expenses from Brandon, Manitoba, to Montreal. That would be comparable to a $2,000 bill today. When asked about his eating habits, Mummery stated he required six meals a day as well as a few snacks, plus a quart of cream to go with every meal. According to old-timers, Mummery's food bills have never been matched.

Aside from active players in the NHL, can you name the only point scoring champion not to be inducted into the Hockey Hall of Fame?

Herb Cain of Boston, who topped all scorers in 1943–44.

Name the Calder Trophy winner who was on several NHL teams before capturing the award.

Carl Voss, the first winner of the rookie award in 1932–33, was on his third NHL team when he won the Calder. Voss was in 14 games with Toronto spread over two seasons before he scored 8 goals and 15 assists split between the Rangers and Detroit.

Who had the shortest career of all the rookie award winners?

Frank McCool had the shortest big-league career of any Calder winner—two seasons, only one of which was a full campaign.

Have NHL teams ever gone through a season without making any trades?

In 1966–67, according to *The Hockey News*, there were no trades made by the six NHL clubs throughout the season.

Who is the youngest player to take part in a professional game outside the NHL?

In March, 1966, 14-year-old Doug Bentley, Jr., son of the former NHL star, with permission of the league, took part in a game between the Knoxville Knights and the Jacksonville Rockets.

Has a pro team ever mutinied?

Yes. In 1970, when the manager of the Nashville Dixie Flyers in the

Eastern Hockey League fined his players $70 because of poor play against Greensboro, the players mutinied and refused to play. EHL president Tom Lockhart suspended the team for five games and tried to have the players banned from hockey altogether, but was unable to get the backing necessary to do so.

In those Score-O competitions between periods, where fans try to win a major prize by shooting a puck into a tiny slot in a board covering the net, has anyone ever won?

A fellow in Oshawa, Ontario, did. Dave Duncan, 25, won $8,000 toward the purchase of a car between periods of an Oshawa Generals' game when he slid the puck from center ice through a slot slightly larger than the puck. What's truly amazing is that Duncan is legally blind. And in Winnipeg, at a Jets' game, a lady took her shot and the puck dribbled toward the end boards when it collided with another puck left there by the previous shooter. When the crowd yelled, "Give her another chance," authorities did so. You guessed it. Her second shot went right through the slot and she won two cars.

What multi-millionaire jockey used to moonlight as a penalty timekeeper in the NHL?

Jockey Sandy Hawley, an avid hockey fan, often served as penalty timekeeper in the penalty box at the Los Angeles Forum during Kings' games.

Who scored the winning goal in the longest game ever played? What teams were involved?

The playoff game in Montreal between the Montreal Maroons and the Detroit Red Wings in 1936 began at 8:34 p.m. on March 24 and ended at 2:25 a.m. on the 25th, after 116 minutes and 30 seconds of overtime. It was Detroit winger Modere (Mud) Bruneteau who finally ended the marathon. Most of the players were dead on their feet by the time the sixth overtime period began, especially the goalies, Lorne Chabot of the Maroons and Normie Smith of the Red Wings.

Late in the sixth overtime, Red Wings coach Jack Adams sent Bruneteau, a seldom-used forward, over the boards. Bruneteau was surprised. He had played infrequently during the contest. Indeed, he had played in only 24 games during the season and had scored just two goals. Seconds after leaping on the ice, he took a pass, dashed in on Chabot, and scored. Teammates mobbed him and ripped off his jersey. Fans raced onto the ice and began pushing money at him, bills of all denominations. And when he finally got to bed at five in the morning, there was a pounding on his door. It was the losing goalie, Lorne Chabot, holding a puck in his hand. "It's for you, Mud," he said. "I thought you'd like this souvenir of your big goal."

Name the team that had only one victory to show for its history in the NHL.

In the first season of play, 1917–18, the NHL consisted of the Montreal Canadiens, the Montreal Wanderers, the Toronto Arenas and the Ottawa Senators. The Wanderers won their opening game, 10–9, over Toronto, then lost to the Canadiens and twice to Ottawa. On the eve of their fifth game, the Wanderers' arena burned down and they dropped out of the league, never to return. So their NHL record shows one victory and five defeats.

Name the team that had only four victories to show for their stay in the NHL.

In 1930–31, the Philadelphia Quakers had a brief one-year stint in the NHL and finished the season with only four wins in 44 games.

How many scoreless, penalty-free games have been played in the history of the NHL?

Just one. It was played in Chicago on February 20, 1944. The Leafs and the Blackhawks skated to a 0–0 tie that night and not a penalty was called. The game was over in one hour and fifty-five minutes.

Was a fan arrested at a game for throwing a live animal on the ice?

At the Forum in Los Angeles on March 6, 1988, Craig Rodenfels, 30, was arrested on a charge of suspicion of cruelty to animals and malicious mischief after he heaved a live chicken on the ice during a Kings' game.

What wedding bet did Wayne Gretzky lose?

When he was with the Oilers, Wayne bet teammates Kevin Lowe and Mark Messier that he would be the last of the three to get married. In July, 1988, when he was about to marry actress Janet Jones, Wayne paid off the bet—$2000.

What star hockey player's funeral was held in his favorite arena?

When hockey superstar Howie Morenz died on March 8, 1937, his funeral was held at the Montreal Forum. Thousands of fans lined the streets outside in bitterly cold weather. They came to pay their final respects to the game's most dominant player. An estimated 50,000 people filed past his coffin.

Did Harold Ballard once propose that coach Roger Neilson wear a paper bag over his head behind the Leaf bench?

In 1979, Ballard, who fired Neilson two days before the famous "paper bag" incident, secretly rehired him when several Leaf players, led by Darryl Sittler, asked him to. Neilson was back on the payroll, but the fans at Maple Leaf Gardens had no idea who would be coaching the team when the Leafs took the ice for their next home game. Ballard wanted Neilson to make an entrance wearing a paper bag over his head. To his credit, Neilson refused. He received a standing ovation when he appeared.

Has a player in the NHL ever been thrown in jail for his on-ice behavior?

It happened in the summer of 1988. On August 24, Dino Ciccarelli became the first NHLer to be given a jail term for attacking another player on the ice. A Toronto judge sentenced Ciccarelli to one day in the slammer for belting Leaf defenseman Luke Richardson over the head with his hockey stick. The convicted player spent a couple of hours in a cell, during which time he signed autographs for his cellmates. Ciccarelli was also fined $1,000 by the judge. The North Star player had some interesting observations about his experience. "When I walked into the precinct house," he said, "the first thing I saw was a big fat cop eating a jelly doughnut."

How did three NHL coaches get locked in a dressing room during a game?

It happened in Chicago. Between periods of a game between the Blackhawks and the Blues during the 1987–88 season, the Chicago coaches held a strategy meeting in a spare locker room. Blackhawk coach Bob Murdoch, angry over his team's play, slammed the door on his way in and the door locked shut. Workmen couldn't get it open, even using axes. Finally, with the game delayed for five minutes, a forklift truck was brought in to knock the door off its hinges and the coaches were freed.

Who were the last surviving members of the old six-team NHL to play in the 21-team league?

Wayne Cashman, Serge Savard and Carol Vadnais. On April 24, 1983, Wayne Cashman of the Boston Bruins played in his final NHL game, the seventh game of the Boston-Buffalo playoff series that spring. Two weeks earlier, two other surviving members of the six-team circuit played their final games—Serge Savard of the Winnipeg Jets and Carol Vadnais of the New Jersey Devils.

Did an NHL team once threaten to go on strike if a player signed by them was barred from playing?

Yes. In 1976 the Chicago Blackhawks players threatened to go on strike if the Boston Bruins were successful in keeping Bobby Orr off the ice. Bruins' defenseman Orr became a free agent and signed a contract with the Hawks. The Bruins threatened to file suit in U.S. district court for an injunction restraining Orr from playing with Chicago unless the Bruins received "adequate" compensation from the Hawks.

Was a team once fined for waving towels on the bench?

During the 1982 playoffs, the Vancouver Canucks were fined $11,000 by the league for waving white towels tossed over the ends of their hockey sticks. It was an impulsive move by coach Roger Neilson and the Canucks to protest the officiating in their series with Chicago. While the players were forbidden to wave the towels, the fans in Vancouver shelled out $4.95 each to purchase specially marked towels to wave during the remaining games in the series.

How old was Johnny Bower when he made the NHL as a regular with the Leafs?

Nobody knows for certain how old he was, but most figure he was 33. Hockey records show his date of birth as November 8, 1924, in Prince Albert, Saskatchewan, but Bower just smiles when asked if the record is accurate.

At one time did professional hockey experiment with colored pucks?

Yes. The WHA, anxious to make the puck more visible for fans watching on TV, experimented with red, then blue pucks. When players complained that the "painted" pucks took peculiar bounces, the pucks were discarded.

Three times in his career this 50-goal scorer scored number 50 on his birthday. Can you name him?

Phil Esposito. Five times in his career Phil scored 50 or more goals. On three occasions he scored number 50 on February 20th—his birthday.

Did a hockey team once carry an accused bank robber on its roster?

In 1898, a man named Billy Ponton was tried in Napanee, Ontario, for the robbery of the local Dominion Bank. Released on bail of $10,000, Ponton was signed by a Kingston, Ontario, hockey club when it embarked on a tour of western Ontario. Ponton's name and photo appeared on posters advertising the team's schedule. Although his presence attracted fans to the games, he was no star. One reporter wrote: "Ponton was about as active as a wooden post and he spent a bad hour on the ice."

What is the strangest promotion a team has held to attract customers to its games?

One of them would be "Dog Night" in Indianapolis. During the 1988–89 season, the first-year Indianapolis team of the international League attracted a season-high 8,030 people by handing out free hot dogs and dog dishes to the first fans who "barked" their way into the arena. A special discount was given to fans who dressed up as dogs and to those whose names were Spot, Fido, Rover, King or Jimmy.

What NHL player offered a teammate a huge sum of money to give up his sweater number?

When Tiger Williams was traded to Vancouver in 1980 he offered Bob Manno $10,000 for his sweater number—22. Manno declined the offer. A few days later, Manno was sent to the minors and Tiger claimed the number without having to spend a dime for it.

What minor pro team once represented two cities?

The St. Louis Flyers. In the 1930s, when hockey was gaining a foothold in the U.S. Midwest, a team from Wichita, Kansas, was scheduled to open the season but it had no players. So the league president called the owner of the St. Louis Flyers and asked him to send his team to Wichita to represent that city wearing Wichita jerseys. The Flyers' owner complied. A week later, there was another request and again the Flyers represented Wichita. By the third week, the Flyers' owner had had enough. When requested once more to bring his players to Wichita, he had the perfect out. "Can't do it, Mr. President. Our next game is against Wichita!"

Which NHL trainer ran out on the ice in the middle of a Stanley Cup playoff game?

During a game between Los Angeles and Calgary in the 1989 playoffs, goalie Mike Vernon of the Flames was punched in the face by Bernie Nicholls of the Kings. Vernon fell to the ice, apparently unconscious. While the Flames led a rush up the ice, one that resulted in a goal, Bearcat Murray, the Flames' trainer, leaped over the boards and ran across the ice to assist Vernon. None of the officials saw Murray's mad dash so there was no whistle. The Calgary goal counted and Murray bragged later that he was "plus one" for the playoffs.

Did an NHL team once wear white hockey pants?

The 1974–75 Washington Capitals, during their first year in the NHL, included white pants in their first set of road uniforms. But the pants lasted exactly four games. The Caps, arguably hockey's worst ever team, spent so much time on the seat of their new pants, that even the best cleaning establishments couldn't get the stains out and the pants were quickly discarded.

What bizarre ritual took place before Los Angeles Kings' playoff games in 1989?

A local disc jockey in Los Angeles was encouraged to drop his pants and rub his naked butt on the ice at the Great Western Forum prior to each Kings' playoff game. Fortunately, this ritual took place long before the spectators arrived. Owner Bruce McNall was convinced the DJ's "lucky butt" helped the Kings in their playoff battles.

Who was the youngest player to take part in the Stanley Cup playoffs?

On December 19, 1904, 17-year-old Albert Forrest, the goalie on the Dawson City team, began a 4,000-mile trek to Ottawa and a playoff series with the famous Ottawa Silver Seven. Albert and his mates left the Yukon, some walking, others on bicycles. When the bikes broke down, they journeyed by dog sled, stage, boat and train. After 24 days on the road, they arrived in Ottawa without having practiced for almost a month. The young goalie was beaten 9–2 and 23–2 in the series but the spectators praised his brilliance. "If it hadn't been for young Forrest," wrote one reporter, "the score would have been double what it was."

Know Your Arenas

1. The Fleet Center in Boston was constructed quite close to the Old Boston Garden. How close was its nearest wall to the old building?
   a. One mile
   b. One city block
   c. One foot
   d. Nine inches

2. The original home for the St. Louis Blues when they joined the NHL in 1967–68 was an old building called _____.

3. In 1967, NHL president Clarence Campbell called it "a fantastic building, the finest sports emporium in creation." Famous actor Lorne Greene emceed the opening. Name the arena.

4. A big league arena named after a famous boxing champion is located in what city?

5. Four of the NHL arenas are named after major airlines. Name two of them.

6. The only NHL arena with a retractable roof is located in what city?

7. Who plays on the Pond?

8. Name the home of the Tampa Bay Lightning.

9. In 1931, the home of this original six team was built in six months for a mere $1.5 million. Name the building.

10. This former home of an NHL team has been the site of more Stanley Cup triumphs than any other arena.

Answers:
1. *d. Nine inches*
2. *St. Louis Arena*
3. *Los Angeles Forum, later called the Great Western Forum*
4. *Detroit (Joe Louis Arena)*
5. *New Jersey's Continental Airlines Arena, US Airways Arena in Washington, the Air Canada Centre in Toronto and Canadian Airlines Saddledome in Calgary*
6. *Pittsburgh*
7. *The Mighty Ducks of Anaheim*
8. *Ice Palace*
9. *Maple Leaf Gardens*
10. *The Forum in Montreal*

Hockey Math

Try to figure out which position each player plays on the team below. To help you solve the puzzle, use the clues given. Then put an "X" in the chart at each position a player cannot play.

Player	C	LW	RW	LD	RD	G
Michael						
Tony						
Luigi						
Frank						
Sol						
Paul						

Clues:

- Mike, Tony and Sol were born in a different month than the goalie.
- Luigi and Frank are older than the goalie.
- Mike and the right defenseman were not born on the same day.
- Sal and the left winger were not born on the same day.
- Mike is younger than Luigi; Luigi is younger than Sol; Sol is younger than Paul; Paul is younger than Tony. The center is the oldest player on the team.

When you feel sure a player plays a certain position, put an "X" opposite his name in the other positions.

Answer:
C Tony, LW Frank, RW Sol, LD Mike, RD Luigi, G Paul

Hockey Logic

From the standings below, try to figure out the scores of the games that have been played. The first one has been given.

team	gp	w	l	t	pts	gf	ga
Leafs	2	2	0	0	4	8	3
Bruins	2	1	0	1	1	5	3
Sabres	2	0	1	1	1	4	8
Stars	2	0	2	0	0	2	5

Leafs	5	Sabres	1
Sabres	___	Bruins	___
Leafs	___	Stars	___
Bruins	___	Stars	___

Answer:

Sabres	**3**	**Bruins**	**3**
Leafs	**3**	**Stars**	**2**
Bruins	**2**	**Stars**	**0**

What's the Score?

Look at the early season standings. Each team has played each other team once. The Flyers have beaten each opponent by the same score. Study the team standing to discover the scores of all six games.

Team	gp	w	l	t	pts	gf	ga
Flyers	3	3	0	0	6	12	3
Red Wings	3	1	1	1	3	8	6
Rangers	3	0	1	2	2	2	3
Flames	3	0	2	1	1	1	9

Answer:
Flyers beat each team by 4–1
Flames 0 Rangers 0
Red Wings 5 Flames 0
Red Wings 2 Rangers 2

It's a Numbers Game

1. In the sixties this Hall of Famer wore No. 7, No. 16 and then No. 9. Who is he?

2. This future Hall of Famer gave up his No. 7 to a superstar forward and took No. 77 instead.

3. This Hall of Fame goaltender once wore No. 00.

4. Most players avoid No. 13. Not this superstar player with a Canadian team.

5. Name two famous Leafs who wore No. 27.

6. Four Hall of Fame players—a Red Wing, two Habs and a Bruin—made No. 4 famous. Can you name them?

7. The leading scorer in the NHL for the 1997–98 season wore No. ___.

8. The numbers 2, 3, 4, 5, 7, 9 and 15 are the retired numbers of famous players from which NHL club?

9. The New York Rangers have retired only two numbers—1 and 7. Who wore those numbers with distinction?

10. Mark Messier is the only player in team history to wear No. 11 for one of the three NHL teams for whom he's played. Which team is it?

11. The Edmonton Oilers have produced great NHL stars—Gretzky, Messier, Coffey, Lowe, Fuhr. Yet only one Oiler jersey number is retired—number 3. What former Oiler wore this number?

12. Aside from Mario Lemieux's No. 66, the Penguins have retired only one other number, even though the player who wore No. 21 played only one season for the Penguins. Who was he?

13. Who wore the Vancouver Canucks only retired jersey—No. 12?

14. The Leafs list several "honored" numbers but only two retired numbers—5 and 6. No. 5 was killed in a plane crash, No. 6 suffered a career-ending injury in the thirties. Can you name these players?

15. Only one NHL team has retired the jersey numbers of two brothers. Name the team and the brothers.

16. During the 1988–89 season, the Chicago Blackhawks retired sweater numbers belonging to two former goalies. Who were the goalies? What were their numbers?

17. Two players have had their sweater numbers retired by two different NHL clubs. Who are they? What were their clubs?

18. The Leafs retired Ace Bailey's number for many years, but at Bailey's request it was unretired and given to a player Bailey admired, right winger _____.

19. Minnesota retired a number belonging to a player whose career was cut short by an on-ice tragedy. If you recall the number he wore, you're an All-Star. Who was the player?

20. The Philadelphia Flyers have retired four numbers. One belonged to a goalie, the others were worn by a defenseman (deceased), a scorer and a Flyer captain. Can you name all four?

Answers:

1. Bobby Hull, 2. Ray Bourque (to Phil Esposito who coveted No 7. when he was traded to Boston, 3. Bernie Parent, 4. Mats Sundin, 5. Frank Mahovlich and Darryl Sittler, 6. Red Kelly (Detroit), Jean Beliveau and Aurel Joliat (Montreal) and Bobby Orr (Boston). 7. 68 (Jaromir Jagr), 8. Boston (Shore, Hitchman, Orr, Clapper, Esposito, Bucyk and Schmidt), 9. Ed Giacomin (1) and Rod Gilbert (7), 10. Edmonton, 11. Al Hamilton, 12. Michel Briere, who died of injuries suffered in a car accident following his rookie season. 13. Stan Smyl, 14. Bill Barilko and Ace Bailey, 15. Montreal. Maurice (9) and Henri Richard (16). 16. Glenn Hall, No. 1, and Tony Esposito, No. 35. 17. Bobby Hull, No. 9 (Chicago and Winnipeg) and Gordie Howe, No. 9 (Detroit and Hartford). 18. Ron Ellis, 19. Bill Masterton, No. 19, 20. Goalie Bernie Parent (1), defenseman Barry Ashbee (4) and former captain Bobby Clarke (16) and Bill Barber (7).

A Sense of Direction

In recent years, the NHL has taken off in all directions. See if you can identify the team from the geographical or historical clues provided. E.g., Clue: Play in the home of the bean and the cod. A: Boston.

1. After a Cup win in the nineties, the team had no civic celebration because it's not located in a city.

2. The Supremes were discovered here.

3. One mile above sea level at the junction of the S. Platte River and Cherry Creek.

4. County seat of Santa Clara County on the Guadalupe River, eight miles from the Bay.

5. The city's original NHL team was known as the Pirates.

6. Home to the largest library in North America.

7. Was the capital of the United States from 1790 to 1800.

8. A state capital, the city is surrounded by the Salt River Valley, and the Roosevelt Dam is nearby.

9. One-Eyed Frank McGee helped win Stanley Cups here.

10. They dumped tea in the city harbor.

11. The city once had another NHL club named the Eagles.

12. In 1911, two famous hockey brothers built one of the first artificial ice rinks in Canada here.

Answers:
1. New Jersey, 2. Detroit, 3. Denver, 4. San Jose, 5. Pittsburgh, 6. Washington, 7. Philadelphia, 8. Phoenix, 9. Ottawa, 10. Boston, 11. St. Louis, 12. Vancouver.

Some More Tough Questions

The following quiz is for hockey fans who REALLY know the game—and have a gift for recalling trivia.

1. Name the only player who received his full year's salary in 1994–95, the year of the NHL player lockout.

2. The original NHL Players' Association was formed in 1957 with Ted Lindsay as president. Who was vice president?

3. What small town in Nova Scotia bills itself as "the birthplace of hockey"?

4. You probably know that Manon Rheaume was the first woman to be given a tryout by an NHL club and the first woman to play in a pro

game (for the IHL's Atlanta Knights). But another woman goaltender became the first woman to win a game in pro hockey. Who is she?

5. All the record books list Vic Lynn as playing with five of the six Original Six teams. But a call to Lynn in Saskatoon reveals that in 1942, he played in one game with the sixth club, making him the only player in history to play with all six teams. Can you name the team he played for briefly in 1942?

6. In 1983, only three players who'd played with Original Six teams were still active in the NHL. They played with Boston, Winnipeg and New Jersey respectively. Can you name them?

7. During the 1998–99 NHL season, Tim Horton's long standing record for most games played by a defenseman (1,446) was broken by two of the following players:
    a. Ray Bourque b. Al McInnis c. Chris Chelios d. Larry Murphy

8. During his illustrious career, Detroit's Steve Yzerman has captured just one major individual NHL trophy. Which one?

9. Can you name the five Chicago Blackhawks who've had their numbers retired?

10. Seven members of the Boston Bruins have had their numbers retired. Can you name five of them?

Answers:

1. *Mario Lemieux. He declared his back injury before the NHL decided on a lockout, which meant his guaranteed contract was in effect whether games were played or not.*
2. *Doug Harvey of Montreal*
3. *Windsor, Nova Scotia*
4. *Erin Whitten*
5. *New York Rangers, even though he is not listed anywhere in the Ranger records.*
6. *Wayne Cashman, Boston, Serge Savard, Winnipeg, Carol Vadnais, New Jersey*
7. *Larry Murphy (1477 games) and Ray Bourque (1453 games)*
8. *The Conn Smythe Trophy (in 1998)*

9. **Bobby Hull, Stan Mikita, Glenn Hall, Tony Esposito and Denis Savard**
10. **Eddie Shore, Lionel Hitchman, Milt Schmidt, Dit Clapper, Johnny Bucyk, Phil Esposito and Bobby Orr**

The Original Six

How much do you know about the NHL teams known as The Original Six—the Leafs, the Habs, the Red Wings, the Bruins, the Blackhawks and the Rangers?

The Rangers:

1. What Ranger player won the Lady Byng Trophy seven times?

2. This Ranger scored over 400 career goals and was known as hockey's answer to Joe Namath.

3. After retiring from the NHL and after being inducted into the Hockey Hall of Fame, this famous ex-Hab made a comeback with the Rangers in 1988.

4. Who served as captain when the Rangers won the Stanley Cup in 1994?

5. Name the Ranger who was named MVP of the 1994 Stanley Cup playoffs—the first American to capture the Conn Smythe Trophy.

The Red Wings:

1. In 1942, the Red Wings were leading the Stanley Cup final series three games to none when their opponents sprang to life and captured the next four games and the Stanley Cup. It remains a hockey "first." Can you name the team that stunned Detroit?

2. A Red Wing named Howe once scored a modern day record of six goals in a game. Was it Syd Howe, Gordie Howe or Mark Howe?

3. This tough little Red Wing finished second in the individual scoring race in 1956–57. But manager Jack Adams traded him to Chicago

because of his involvement in a fledgling players' association. Can you name him?

4.   In what business did Detroit owner Mike Ilitch make a fortune?

5.   True or false? Gordie Howe never enjoyed a 100-point season as a Red Wing.

The Habs

1.   For 12 seasons during the fifties and sixties the Montreal Canadiens kept the same three centermen in their lineup. Can you name them?

2.   Goalie Ken Dryden is well known for leading the Habs to the Stanley Cup in 1971 and winning the Calder Trophy the following year. But two other Habs won Calder Trophies, with other NHL clubs, a year after celebrating a Montreal Stanley Cup triumph. Can you name them?

3.   A Montreal player is the only non–Hall of Famer to play on nine Stanley Cup championship teams. Do you recall his name?

4.   This little goalie chalked up 75 shutouts in seven seasons of NHL play with Montreal. He still holds the record for most shutouts in a season, set in 1928–29. Name him.

5.   To what poem do the words "To you from failing hands we throw the torch; be yours to hold it high" belong?

The Bruins:

1.   This Boston employee became the first man in NHL history to record 1,000 victories as general manager.

2.   True or false? Joe Thornton and Sergei Samsonov were drafted No. 1 and No. 8 respectively in the 1997 NHL entry draft.

3. In their history, the Bruins have been guided by how many general managers?
   a. ten
   b. five
   c. fifteen

4. In what season did the Bruins last win the Stanley Cup?

5. Name the Bruin who played the longest and scored the most goals in a Boston uniform.

The Blackhawks

1. True or false? A former NHL referee and major league baseball umpire once coached the Blackhawks to the Stanley Cup.

2. How many Stanley Cups have the Blackhawks won?
   a. three
   b. five
   c. seven

3. Who scored more goals as a Blackhawk—Stan Mikita or Bobby Hull?

4. Who coached the Blackhawks to a Stanley Cup in 1961?

5. From 1982–83 to 1992–93, this Blackhawk played in 884 consecutive games. Can you name him?

The Leafs:

1. Who was the general manager of the Leafs before Ken Dryden?

2. In February, 1960, the Leafs traded a journeyman defenseman to Detroit for a future Hall of Famer who helped lead the Leafs to four Stanley Cups. Can you name the two players involved in this famous deal?

3. Who holds the record for most career points as a Leaf?
   a. Borje Salming
   b. Darryl Sittler
   c. George Armstrong

4. Darryl Sittler once scored a record 10 points in a game versus Boston. Did he score:
   a. 5 goals and 5 assists
   b. 6 goals and four assists
   c. 4 goals and 6 assists

5. Who coached the Leafs to their last Stanley Cup in 1967?
   a. Hap Day
   b. Joe Primeau
   c. Punch Imlach

Answers:

Rangers:
1. Frank Boucher, 2. Rod Gilbert, 3. Guy Lafleur, 4. Mark Messier, 5. Brian Leetch.

Red Wings:
1. Toronto, 2. Syd Howe, 3. Ted Lindsay, 4. Pizza, 5. False. Howe tallied 103 points in 1968–69, his only 100-point season as a Red Wing.

Habs:
1. Beliveau, H. Richard, Backstrom 2. Danny Grant ('68) and Tony Esposito ('69,) 3. Claude Provost, 4. George Hainsworth, 5. "In Flanders Fields".

Bruins:
1. Harry Sinden, 2. True, 3. b. Five, 4. 1971–72, 5. Johnny Bucyk (21 seasons, 545 goals).

Blackhawks:
1. True. Bill Stewart coached the Hawks to the 1938 Stanley Cup.
2. a. Three, 3. Bobby Hull (604 to 541), 4. Rudy Pilous, 5. Steve Larmer.

Leafs:
1. Cliff Fletcher, 2. Marc Reaume and Red Kelly, 3. b. Darryl Sittler (916 points), 4. b. 6 goals and 4 assists, 5. Punch Imlach.

They're Paying Him How Much?

Salaries are soaring in the NHL and it's hard to keep track of who makes what. Using figures released at the start of the 1998–99 season by *The Hockey News*, we've compiled the following quiz. All figures are in U.S. dollars.

1. In 1998–99, Detroit's Sergei Fedorov was the NHL's top money earner at $14 million ($2 million in base salary and a $12 million signing bonus. How much did team captain Steve Yzerman earn? Was it $10 million, $8.5 million or $4.8 million?

2. If the Mighty Ducks' Paul Kariya earned $8.5 million in 1998–99, how much did teammate Teemu Selanne get paid? Was it $4.75 million, $10 million or $8.5 million?

3. If Buffalo's Dominik Hasek earned $8 million, how much did Colorado's Patrick Roy earn? Was it $12.5 million, $8.5 million or $5.11 million?

4. If Colorado's Peter Forsberg earned $6 million, how much did Brett Hull of the Dallas Stars earn? Was it $6 million, $8.5 million or $4.5 million?

5. If Doug Gilmour of Chicago earned $6 million, how much did Wayne Gretzky earn? Was it $12 million, $6 million or $4.5 million?

6. Here's an unusual deal. Which NHL star's salary was based on the average of the top three salaries in the league, which was calculated at $10.33 million? Was it:
    a. Pavel Bure b. Jaromir Jagr c. Mike Modano

7. According to *The Hockey News*, the highest-paid NHL coach in 1998–99 was
    a. Pat Burns b. Pat Quinn c. Scotty Bowman d. Marc Crawford

8. The highest paid coach, according to *The Hockey News*, signed a contract calling for
   a. $1.1 million for four years b. $750,000 for two years c. $950,000 for 5 years

9. Coaching salaries have risen by what percentage in the past three seasons?
   a. 10% b. 36% c. 54%

10. The average coaching salary in the NHL (for the 1998–99 season) was calculated at:
    a. $400,000 b. $650,000 c. $593,000

Answers:

1. $4.8 million, 2. $4.75 million, 3. $5.11 million, 4. $4.5 million, 5. $6 million, 6. Pavel Bure, 7. Pat Quinn, 8. $1.1 million for four years. (Note: Marc Crawford signed with Vancouver in mid-season for a reported $1.1 million for three years and Quinn received a salary boost when he took on the additional role of GM following the 1998-99 season), 9. 54% 10. $593,000.

More on Salaries

Can you explain why the Detroit Red Wings payroll leaped by almost $20 million in 1998–99 while the Colorado Avalanche spent over $12 million less during the same season?

Detroit's payroll took a leap because the Carolina Hurricanes made a stunning offer sheet to Sergei Fedorov which the Wings felt compelled to match. Fedorov received $12 million in signing bonus and $2 million in salary. In the previous season, the Rangers made an even bigger offer to Joe Sakic—a $15 million bonus and $2 million in salary which the Avs decided to match. With the $15 million behind them, the Avs payroll plummeted by $12.3 million in 1998–99.

Was Pittsburgh's Jaromir Jagr on the list of the top ten highest-paid players in 1998–99? If not, why not?

Jagr was not on the top ten list. But he will be in 1999–2000 when his salary of $4.9 million nearly doubles to $8.9 million.

How much do the Pittsburgh Penguins owe retired superstar Mario Lemieux in deferred salary?

Estimates range from $27 million to more than $31 million.

Did all NHL teams in 1998-99 have at least one million dollar player on the roster?

Yes. Nashville had just one in their first season—Tom Fitzgerald, who signed as a free agent for $1.6 million. Was he worth it? Fitzgerald, who never compiled more than 40 points in any of his 10 NHL previous seasons, finished 6th (32 points) in team scoring.

Did any team have a "bargain-of-the-year" player in 1998–99?

Yes. The Carolina Hurricanes inked goaltender Arturs Irbe to a two-year contract at $550,000 per season. And goalie Ron Tugnutt of Ottawa was a bargain at $552,500.

Which NHL player donated a large portion of his salary to charity in 1998–99?

In February, 1999, Detroit star Sergei Fedorov donated $2 million to endow the Fedorov Foundation. Using Fedorov's funds, a day camp was established to help autistic and developmentally handicapped children in southeastern Michigan. Another program funded a college scholarship to a deserving student from an at-risk environment. Fedorov also donated $91 dollars to charity for every goal the Red Wings scored for the rest of the season.

Player Pay

We all know players salaries have skyrocketed in the nineties but how closely do you keep track?

The following quiz will test your knowledge of players' paychecks. Thanks to *The Hockey News* for the info on money matters. All salaries are in U.S. funds and were obtained at the start of the 1998–99 season. Player compensation includes base salary, signing or reporting bonus and deferred income allocated to 1998–99.

Who makes more money?

1. Doug Gilmour or Tony Amonte?
2. Mats Sundin or Curtis Joseph?
3. Phil Housley or Theo Fleury?
4. Peter Forsberg or Patrick Roy?
5. Joe Sakic or Claude Lemieux?
6. Paul Kariya or Teemu Selanne?
7. Sergei Fedorov or Steve Yzerman?
8. Wayne Gretzky or Mark Messier?
9. Wendel Clark or Darren Puppa?
10. Keith Primeau or Ron Francis?

Answers:
1. *Gilmour ($6 million to Amonte's $2.8 million)*
2. *Sundin ($6,347,164 to Joseph's $5.5 million)*
3. *Housley ($2.75 million to Fleury's $2.4 million)*
4. *Forsberg ($6 million to Roy's $5,113,260)*
5. *Lemieux ($2,359,180 to Sakic's $2 million)*
6. *Kariya ($8.5 million to Selanne's $4.75 million)*
7. *Fedorov ($14 million to Yzerman's $4.8 million)*
8. *Gretzky $6 million, Messier $6 million—a tie*
9. *Puppa ($2.3 million to Clark's $1.4 million)*
10. *Francis ($5 million to Primeau's $2 million)*

I'll name the NHL goalies. You tell me how much he earns.

a. $2–3 million   b. $3–4 million   c. $4–5 million   d. Over $5 million

1. Mike Richter   a. ___ b. ___ c. ___ d. ___
2. Dominik Hasek   a. ___ b. ___ c. ___ d. ___
3. Bill Ranford   a. ___ b. ___ c. ___ d. ___
4. Grant Fuhr   a. ___ b. ___ c. ___ d. ___
5. John Vanbiesbrouck   a. ___ b. ___ c. ___ d. ___

Answers:
1. *d. $5.1 million*   2. *d. $8 million*
3. *b. $3,087,344*   4. *b. $3.1 million*
5. *b. $3.5 million*

More About Money

1. Believe it or not, one NHL team paid one of its players more money in 1998–99 than the entire payroll of another NHL team. Can you name the teams and the player who received this whopping salary?

2. The average salary for an NHL player in 1998–99 was:
   a. $950,000 b. $1 million c. $1.2 million d. $2 million

3. Who is the top salaried player in the history of the Edmonton Oilers?
   a. Mark Messier b. Wayne Gretzky c. Doug Weight

4. True or false? No NHL player earned less than $100,000 in 1998–99.

5. The number of millionaires in the NHL in 1998–99 was
   a. 75 b. 160 c. 244 d. 375

6. How many players earned in excess of $5 million in 1998–99?
   a. 7 b. 14 c. 21

7. A veteran center scored just 13 goals in 1997–98 and was outscored by 25 other centers. Even so, as a free agent, he signed a three-year contract with Chicago for $18 million. Can you name him and his team?

8. John LeClair, with three consecutive 50 goal seasons behind him, and a salary of $3,644,975, was out-salaried in 1998–99 by how many of the following NHLers?
   a. Joe Murphy, Sharks, b. Uwe Krupp, Red Wings, c. Steve Duchesne, Kings

9. Which NHL team spent the most money on player salaries in 1998–99?
   a. New York b. Detroit c. Colorado

10. Can you name the goaltender who earns the highest salary in NHL history?

11. In 1968–69 the NHL introduced a standard per diem for players on road trips of $15 per day. How much is it today?

12. In 1921, the Montreal Canadiens' franchise was sold to local sportsmen Joe Cattarinich and Leo Dandurand for what was called "a staggering amount." How much did they pay for it?
a. $11,000 b. $21,000 c. $111,000

Answers:

1. **The Detroit Red Wings paid Sergei Fedorov $14 million, more than the entire payroll ($13.6 million) of the Nashville Predators.**
2. **c. $1.2 million**
3. **c. Doug Weight ($7.75 million over two years)**
4. **False. Steve Leach of Ottawa earned $97,500 in 1998–99. All others earned over $100,000.**
5. **c. 244**
6. **b. 14**
7. **Doug Gilmour. With the Chicago Blackhawks.**
8. **All of them. Murphy ($3.8 million), Krupp ($4.1 million) Duchesne ($3.75 million)**
9. **b. Detroit ($48.3 million)**
10. **Dominik Hasek ($8 million)**
11. **$70.^{00}**
12. **a. $11,000**

At the Draft

1. The first draft of amateur players in the NHL took place in 1963 when 21 players were taken by the six NHL teams. Can you name the first player selected? Was it:
   a. Walt McKechnie
   b. Pete Mahovlich
   c. Gary Monahan

2. In the 1964 amateur draft, a young goaltender from the Etobicoke junior B team was selected by Boston with their third pick. Was he:
   a. Gerry Cheevers
   b. Ken Dryden
   c. Doug Favell

3. In the sixties, the chances of finding a gem at the draft table were slim. But in 1966, the Rangers got lucky and drafted a future Hall of Fame defenseman. Was he:
   a. Harry Howell
   b. Jim Neilson
   c. Brad Park

4. In 1969, the Montreal Canadiens exercised a special option to select two French Canadian players before any others amateur stars were drafted. Can you name the players they chose? Were they:
   a. Pierre Bouchard and Mario Tremblay
   b. Rejean Houle and Marc Tardif
   c. Patrick Roy and Vincent Damphousse

5. As newcomers to the NHL in 1970, Buffalo and Vancouver enjoyed the first two draft selections. A spin of the wheel gave the Sabres first choice and general manager Punch Imlach selected a future Hall of Famer. Can you name him?

6. In the 1970 draft, Montreal selected goaltender Ray Martiniuk (No. 5 overall) but in the same draft they could have chosen another goalie who went on to a Hall of Fame career. The goalie the Habs ignored was drafted No. 59 by Los Angeles. Was he:
   a. Dan Bouchard
   b. Billy Smith
   c. Bernie Parent

7. In the 1974 draft, Punch Imlach of the Buffalo Sabres concocted a major practical joke by drafting a mythical Japanese player. He plucked a name from the Buffalo telephone book and claimed the unknown Asian player was a star on the Tokyo Katanas team. Do you remember the player's name? Was it
   a. Taro Tsujimoto
   b. Taro Kamamoto
   c. Taro Kimona

8. This player from Sweden was passed over for three years before being drafted 133rd overall in 1994. In the 1995–96 season he led his

NHL team in scoring and won the Calder Trophy. Is he
a. Mats Sundin
b. Daniel Alfredsson
c. Peter Forsberg

9. Calder Trophy winner Gary Suter was selected by the Calgary Flames in the 1984 draft. Was he taken
a. In the first round
b. In the second round
c. After 100 others were selected

10. In 1982, the New Jersey Devils were so anxious to draft the kid brother of a famous Islander (an Art Ross, Hart and Conn Smythe Trophy winner) that they traded star defenseman Rob Ramage to St. Louis in order to obtain a more favorable draft position. They got their man, but the kid brother never amounted to much and played in only 38 NHL games. Can you name him?

11. When the Montreal Canadiens selected Doug Wickenheiser as the first overall draft pick in 1980 they were criticized for not choosing a Montreal native who went on to become one of the top scorers in NHL history. Can you name him?

12. Mario Lemieux was Pittsburgh's first choice (and first overall) in 1984. But a player drafted 117th by Calgary in the '84 draft emerged as a sniper almost equal to Lemieux. He captured the Hart Trophy in 1991, the season he set a record for goals by a right winger with 86. Can you name him?

13. In 1986, for the first time in draft history, a U.S. college star was selected first overall by Detroit. Can you name him?

14. With players like Pierre Turgeon, Brendan Shanahan and Joe Sakic available in the 1987 draft, a small man had to wait his turn and hope for the best. Calgary waited until the ninth round to select this 5'6" forward (166th overall) and they were amazed at how quickly he fit in. Can you name him?

15. In 1988, Minnesota selected an American player from Livonia,

Michigan, with the No. 1 draft pick. He was runner-up to Sergei Makarov for the Calder Trophy in 1990. Most fans thought he should have won the Calder because Makarov was a 31-year-old veteran of Russian hockey. Can you name him?

16. In 1991, the player drafted first overall refused to join the team that drafted him. The team finally traded him—to two other teams. It took an arbitrator to straighten things out. Can you name him?

17. In 1992, the Tampa Bay Lightning proudly drafted the kid brother of an NHL superstar. But the brother scored only one goal in his brief NHL career. Can you name him?

18. In 1992, the Flyers had high hopes for the kid brother of a former Flyer and Maple Leaf. They selected him No. 7 overall. He never played a game in the NHL. Can you name him?

19. The Boston Bruins had two first round draft choices in 1997. Their second choice, Sergei Samsonov, won rookie of the year honors in 1998. Can you name Boston's first choice in '97?

20. At the draft in Buffalo in 1998, Vincent Lecavalier was drafted first overall by Tampa Bay. But who was the second selection, a U.S.-born prospect taken by Nashville?

Answers:

1. *Gary Monahan (by Montreal) Mahovlich went second, McKechnie sixth.*
2. *Ken Dryden*
3. *Brad Park*
4. *Rejean Houle and Marc Tardif*
5. *Gilbert Perreault*
6. *Billy Smith*
7. *Taro Tsujimoto*
8. *Daniel Alfredsson*
9. *Hull was picked 117th, Suter 180th*
10. *Rocky Trottier, brother to Bryan*
11. *Denis Savard*
12. *Brett Hull*
13. *Joe Murphy of Michigan State*
14. *Theoron Fleury*

15. **Mike Modano**
16. **Eric Lindros.** *He refused to join the Quebec Nordiques and they finally made deals for him with both New York Rangers and Philadelphia involving many players. An arbitrator ruled in favor of Philadelphia.*
17. **Brent Gretzky**
18. **Ryan Sittler**
19. **Joe Thornton**
20. **David Legwand**

Did an NHL team ever refuse to take part in the annual draft?

Yes. In 1983, the St. Louis Blues either refused or were not prepared to take part in the draft proceedings because the NHL turned down a St. Louis bid to move to Saskatoon. As it turned out, the Blues didn't lose too much. They had already traded away their first two picks (New Jersey took John MacLean with one, Montreal claimed Sergio Momesso with the other) in earlier deals.

In 1984, when Mario Lemieux was available in the draft, was there a perception that New Jersey and Pittsburgh battled each other for last place overall in order to grab Lemieux?

Yes, that perception existed. After all, the Pens were 3–16–1 in their last 20 games. What's more, the Pens traded their top defenseman, Randy Carlyle, just before the trade deadline and sent highly regarded goalie Roberto Romano to the minors. At the time, the Devils hinted that Pittsburgh might be thinking more of landing Lemieux than winning games. New Jersey, meanwhile, went 4–14–2 in the final 20 games and finished three points ahead of the Pens, who happily grabbed Lemieux.

In 1982, Brian Bellows was the most sought-after junior hockey star in North America. The Boston Bruins had first choice in the draft that year. Why didn't they take Bellows?

Before the draft, the Bruins' Harry Sinden huddled with Lou Nanne of the North Stars. Sinden agreed to pass on Bellows, allowing the North Stars to claim him, if Nanne would give the Bruins two players, left winger Brad Palmer and center Dave Donnelly. Nanne agreed and was overjoyed to get Bellows in the draft. Sinden said later he would have passed on Bellows anyway even if he hadn't made the deal with Nanne. He had already decided to select defenseman Gord Kluzak.

Do many players chosen late in the entry draft blossom into big-league stars?

Not many, but a few "late bloomers" have achieved stardom. Mark Messier, for example, was the 48th choice in '79, Keith Acton 103rd in '78, Pete Peeters 135th in '77 and Dave Taylor 210th in '75.

What action prompted professional hockey teams to begin drafting and signing 18-year-old players?

In 1978, John Bassett, Jr., owner of the Birmingham Bulls of the WHA, went to court when the league refused to accept the contract of Ken Linseman, an under-age player Bassett had signed the previous season. The judge ruled that Linseman could not be denied the right to play pro hockey. The judge's ruling changed hockey dramatically. Bassett signed seven juniors in all—goaltender Pat Riggin, forwards Keith Crowder, Rick Vaive and Michel Goulet, and defensemen Craig Hartsburg, Gaston Gingras and Rob Ramage. Cincinnati signed Mike Gartner and Indianapolis grabbed 17-year-old Wayne Gretzky.

Did a professional hockey team once draft a state governor?

Yes. When the WHA held its first-ever draft, Wendell Anderson, the governor of Minnesota, was drafted by the Minnesota Fighting Saints. The governor was a former college star who helped the U.S. Olympic team win a silver medal at the 1956 Olympic Games. Governor Anderson, while flattered to be drafted, never played for the Fighting Saints.

How did the Montreal Canadiens get the rights to Guy Lafleur and Ken Dryden?

In 1970, general manager Sam Pollock quietly traded Ernie Hicke and the Canadiens' No. 1 draft pick to the Oakland Seals in exchange for Francois Lacombe and the Seals' No. 1 draft choice the following season. When Oakland finished the 1970–71 season with the NHL's worst record, Pollock used the No. 1 pick he'd acquired to draft Lafleur.

In 1964, after Boston drafted Ken Dryden as a 16-year-old amateur, Pollock traded draft choice Guy Allen and Paul Reid to the Bruins in exchange for the pro rights to Dryden and Alex Campbell. The other players faded away but Dryden, after a brilliant career in U.S. college hockey, went on to become a goaltending superstar.

Why was Montreal allowed to draft the two best French-Canadian players available in the sixties?

In 1967, at the request of the NHL Board of Governors, Montreal GM Sam Pollock helped organize plans for all the drafts as the league doubled in size from six to twelve teams. As part of the expansion agreement, Pollock convinced his rivals he should be allowed to draft the two best French-Canadian juniors for a period of 2 years. He used this so-called Pollock Amendment to draft Mark Tardif and Rejean Houle from the Montreal Junior Canadiens in 1969.

Famous Trades

1. One of the biggest trades in hockey history saw Wayne Gretzky move from the Edmonton Oilers to the Los Angeles Kings in return for Jimmy Carson. There were other players and draft choices involved plus a bundle of cash. How much cash did Oiler owner Peter Pocklington, the man who engineered the deal, receive?

2. One of the most disastrous deals the Chicago Blackhawks ever made was trading Phil Esposito, Ken Hodge and Fred Stanfield to Boston in 1967 in return for a forward, a defenseman and a minor league goalie. Can you name the three players Chicago acquired?

3. Nine years after joining Boston, Phil Esposito was dealt to the New York Rangers, along with Carol Vadnais. Two of the Ranger's biggest stars came to Boston in the deal, along with a little-known defenseman. Can you name the new Bruins?

4. Here's a strange one. On June 18, 1987, the New York Rangers traded their No. 1 draft choice and tossed in $100,000 for a man who hadn't scored a goal or an assist for years. Who did they get?

5. Leaf manager Punch Imlach made a brilliant move in 1960. He acquired a veteran defenseman from Detroit, converted him to a centerman and smiled as the new Leaf helped Toronto win four Stanley Cups. Who was the newcomer? Who did Imlach give up in the deal?

6. During his second stint with Toronto as general manager, Punch Imlach traded a popular right winger and a young defenseman to the Colorado Rockies in return for Pat Hickey and Wilf Paiement. The Leaf players were furious at Imlach for making the deal and ripped their dressing room apart in protest. Who were the two Leafs involved in the deal?

7. In June, 1990, the Chicago Blackhawks traded a player who had given them five 100-point seasons in 10 years. He went to Montreal in exchange for a defenseman who went on to capture two Norris Trophies with his new team. Can you name the players involved?

8. On October 10, 1984, this veteran Flyer was told he was about to be named his team's new captain at a press conference. Before he could make his acceptance speech he was told to go home and pack. He'd just been traded to Detroit. Who was he?

9. In 1992, the Blackhawks sent a goaltender they didn't want to Buffalo in return for a goalie named Stephan Beauregard and a fourth round draft choice. The goalie the Hawks dumped went on to win two MVP awards and many other honors with the Sabres. Surely you know his name.

10. In 1992, Toronto manager Cliff Fletcher snared Doug Gilmour from Calgary in a deal that paid big dividends for the Leafs. Calgary counted heavily on a former 51-goal scorer acquired in the trade to be an offensive threat but the player scored a mere 11 goals in 59 games as a Flame, then was dealt to Montreal. Who was he?

11. When Philadelphia acquired Eric Lindros from Quebec in a multi-player deal in 1992, one of the players the Flyers gave up was their top draft choice in 1991. He went on to capture the Calder Trophy as a Nordique. Can you name him?

12. After being traded from Vancouver to Boston in June, 1986, this power forward blossomed into one of the NHL's top scorers. He retired in 1996 with 395 career goals. Who is he? And who was the Bruin who went to Vancouver in the exchange?

Answers:

1. **$15 million**
2. **Pit Martin, Gilles Marotte and (goalie) Jack Norris**
3. **Brad Park, Jean Ratelle and Joe Zanussi**
4. **They got a new coach—Michel Bergeron, from Quebec**
5. **Red Kelly, Marc Reaume**
6. **Lanny McDonald and Joel Quenneville**
7. **Denis Savard and Chris Chelios**
8. **Darryl Sittler, who was dealt for Murray Craven and Joe Paterson**
9. **Dominik Hasek**
10. **Gary Leeman**
11. **Peter Forsberg**
12. **Cam Neely, Barry Pederson**

Chargcters iN the Game

Who was the player known as "Batman"?

In a 1975 Stanley Cup final in Buffalo between Buffalo and Philadelphia, a bat flew over the players' heads midway through the first period. On a face-off, Sabre forward Jim Lorentz swatted the bat with his stick and killed it. The bat lay on the ice and nobody wanted anything to do with it until Rick MacLeish of the Flyers picked it up in his bare hand and took it to the penalty box. Lorentz got plenty of critical mail after the incident. People wrote asking if he wasn't ashamed of himself. One man wanted to take him to court and hoped he'd get a jail sentence for what he'd done. And, of course, from then on he was known as "Batman."

Who uttered the line: "I went to the fights the other night and a hockey game broke out"?

It's one of comedian (and hockey fan) Rodney Dangerfield's most famous lines. Rodney has never played the game, nor does he plan to. "I'd like to play," he says, "but I'm injury-prone. The other day I hurt myself playing Simon Says!"

What famous star wore Groucho Marx glasses and nose on his wedding day?

When Pat LaFontaine of the Islanders and his bride Marybeth made their entrance at their wedding reception, guests in the ballroom broke up. The bride and groom both wore false noses and glasses synonymous with Groucho Marx.

Did a star hockey player once score a goal while skating backwards?

In 1910, Cyclone Taylor, one of hockey's biggest stars, was playing for Renfrew, a town in the Ottawa Valley. Taylor is said to have boasted that he would score a goal while skating backwards against his former club from Ottawa. In the last game of the season, Renfrew walloped Ottawa 17–2. At one point in the game Taylor took a pass from Lester Patrick, spun around skating backwards, and flipped the puck past Percy Lesueur, the Ottawa netminder.

What player angered his team's owners by selling the new station wagon they'd given him to the team's play-by-play broadcaster?

After Red Berenson of the St. Louis Blues scored six goals in a game against Philadelphia in 1968, he was rewarded with a new station wagon. But the team owners were miffed when Berenson promptly sold the car to Blues' broadcaster Dan Kelly.

Only once in NHL history has a player scored 60 goals in a season and not been selected for either the first or second All-Star teams. Who was the overlooked player?

During the 1981–82 season, Dennis Maruk of the Washington Capitals registered 60 goals but finished fourth among centers in the All-Star balloting behind Wayne Gretzky, Bryan Trottier and Peter Stastny.

Who was the first native New Yorker to play for the New York Rangers?

Ever heard of goalie Joe Schaefer? When he finally got his chance to play for the Rangers he was 35 years old, a vice president of a printing company and a veteran of exactly one game in the American Hockey League. Schaefer's job, you see, was to serve as an emergency goalie at Ranger games. If one of the two goalies in the game was injured, he'd go in as a substitute. He waited almost 10 years before he got his chance. Ranger goalie Gump Worsley was injured in a game against Chicago on February 17, 1960. Schaefer played the remaining 39 minutes and 27 seconds to become the first New Yorker to play for his hometown hockey team. A year later, he played in his second game, also against Chicago. His career stats: 86 minutes and 18 seconds of NHL play, no wins, 44 saves and eight goals against.

Is it true that Don Cherry put a teammate up for the night—in his daughter's crib?

In his book *Grapes*, Don Cherry tells how Ranger goalie Gump Worsley was sent down to Springfield as a disciplinary measure. Cherry, then a Springfield player, invited Worsley home for the night, but not until they'd had a few beers. Don's wife Rose had daughter Cindy with her in the main bedroom so Cindy's crib was empty. That was good enough for Worsley. He curled up in the crib and fell asleep.

Has a player in the NHL ever scored 50 goals for two different teams?

Yes. Wayne Gretzky has had 50-goal seasons with Edmonton and Los Angeles. Pierre Larouche was the first to do it, scoring 50 or more with Pittsburgh and Montreal.

Has a player ever led the NHL in scoring while performing for a last-place team?

The first player to do it was Sweeney Schriner of the New York Americans in 1936–37. The second was Max Bentley of Chicago in 1946–47.

Did Montreal coach Toe Blake really punch a referee after a playoff game?

He did indeed. On March 26, 1961, the Canadiens, gunning for a sixth straight Stanley Cup, opened their playoff series with Chicago. In game three, the Hawks held a 1–0 lead until Henri Richard tied the score with 16 seconds to play to send the game into overtime. In the second overtime period, Donnie Marshall batted the puck into the net and claimed the game-winner, but referee Dalt MacArthur waved off the goal. Marshall's stick, ruled the ref, was over his shoulder when he connected. Montreal coach Toe Blake was livid. In the third overtime period the Habs' Dickie Moore took a penalty, and seconds later Murray Balfour scored to win the game. While Chicago fans howled in glee, Blake bolted from behind the Montreal bench, slid across the ice, and walloped the referee with a punch that landed on his shoulder and deflected up to the jaw. Blake not only lost the game (and eventually the series) but his assault on MacArthur cost him a $2,000 fine.

...yne Gretzky once describe a rival team as a "Mickey ...se outfit"?

Yes. In 1983, after the Edmonton Oilers thrashed the New Jersey Devils 13–4, Gretzky ripped into the opposing team. "It's not funny," said Gretzky. "These guys are ruining hockey. They better get their act together. They are putting a Mickey Mouse operation on the ice." Gretzky later apologized to the Devils and their fans.

What is the story behind Pat Verbeek's thumb?

During an off season, Verbeek's left thumb was severed in a corn-planting machine on his farm near Forest, Ontario. The severed thumb was found by Verbeek's father in a bag of fertilizer. He rushed to the hospital where Pat was being treated. Surgeons re-attached the thumb but didn't give much hope of success. But by training camp, Verbeek's thumb looked remarkably healthy. Said Pat, "I think it's even grown a bit. Probably because of all that fertilizer it fell in."

Did an NHL star once launch a multi-million dollar lawsuit against an equipment manufacturer for an injury suffered in a game?

Yes. Defenseman Mark Howe filed a $5 million lawsuit seeking damages for an accident that happened while he was a member of the Hartford Whalers. He sued the Jayfro Corp. of Waterford, Connecticut, the equipment manufacturer, the city of Hartford and the Hartford Civic Centre and Coliseum Authority. Howe suffered a rare and dangerous puncture wound when he slid into a sharp metal goalpost support. Fortunately, he recovered from the career-threatening injury.

Why did transplanted Canadian Jack Kent Cooke sell the L.A. Kings in 1979?

Cooke needed the money. He sold his Los Angeles holdings—the Forum, the Los Angeles Lakers of the National Basketball Association and the Kings—for $67.5 million to help pay for a divorce settlement from his wife Jean. Judge Wapner, later a TV personality on *People's Court*, awarded Mrs. Cooke half of Mr. Cooke's $82 million in assets and the couple's Bel Air estate. Cooke would later call the divorce "the biggest mistake of my life."

Did Bobby Hull end his career in the NHL or the WHA?

The NHL. Bobby had hoped to end his career in Chicago when the NHL merged with four WHA clubs, but Winnipeg general manager John Ferguson drafted Hull for the NHL Jets during the 1979–80 season. He played 18 games with the Jets, then retired. He surfaced with the Hartford Whalers in February, 1980, and played nine games on the same team with Gordie Howe, another hockey legend. Hull stopped playing when his lady friend was seriously injured in a car accident. A year later, Hull joined the New York Rangers for their training camp, but a decision was made not to sign him. He then retired for good.

Was a famous NHL owner once kidnapped and held as a hostage?

During the 1981–82 playoffs, Edmonton Oilers' millionaire owner Peter Pocklington emerged from a bizarre 12-hour hostage-taking drama in his own home with a bullet wound in his arm but his life intact. Pocklington survived the ordeal during which an unemployed 29-year-old Edmonton man held him hostage and demanded $1 million in ransom money. Police ended the ordeal when they stormed the house and fired shots, hitting both Pocklington and the gunman.

Who was the hockey star who hit Leaf owner Harold Ballard in the face with a slapshot?

Bobby Hull. In 1966–67 during the semifinals between the Leafs and the Hawks, Hull took a slapshot in the pre-game warmup. The shot sailed over the end boards and into Ballard's private bunker. It struck Ballard in the nose, breaking it in four places.

Has a woman ever bossed an NHL hockey club?

Yes. In 1954, long before women's liberation began pushing the rights of the fair sex, Marguerite Norris was president of the Detroit Red Wings.

Who were the hockey heroes made honorary members of the Montreal Fire Department?

Several members of the Montreal Canadiens alerted guests and, in doing so, possibly saved several lives in a hotel fire in St. Louis on March 10, 1972. Montreal coach Scotty Bowman's life was in jeopardy until some of his players escorted him to safety. As a result, Pierre Bouchard, J.C. Tremblay, Serge Savard, Guy Lapointe, Dale Hoganson and Rejean Houle won several honors. They were also made honorary members of the Montreal Fire Department.

Which famous star was almost killed in a game early in his career?

In 1950, Gordie Howe was playing for Detroit against Toronto in the Stanley Cup semifinals. In the second period of the first game, Gordie collided heavily with Leaf captain Ted Kennedy near the boards. Unconscious, Howe was carried off on a stretcher and preliminary examinations brought discouraging conclusions. Howe suffered a fractured nose, a deep cut near the eye and a possible fractured skull. A team of doctors performed an emergency operation on his head and this probably saved Howe's life. In a few days he was on his way to complete recovery.

What were the details of the Ted Green/Wayne Maki stick-swinging episode that almost cost Green his life?

During a meaningless pre-season game in Ottawa between Boston and St. Louis on September 21, 1969, Ted Green of the Bruins and Wayne Maki of the Blues were involved in a stick-swinging battle. Hit by Maki's stick, Green was rushed to the hospital and a five-hour brain operation followed. Later, there was additional surgery and a steel plate was imbedded in Green's skull. Maki's suspension was for 30 days, Green's for 13 games if and when he returned to hockey. Assault charges were laid against both players, the first in hockey history. Both men were exonerated in Ottawa court hearings and Green returned to hockey a year later. Maki died of a brain tumor in 1974—a strange coincidence.

How many players have been barred from hockey for life?

Over the years many players have been suspended from hockey for various reasons but only four have been given lifetime suspensions. In a Stanley Cup playoff game between Boston and Ottawa in 1927, Bill Couture (a.k.a. Coutu) of Boston assaulted referee Jerry Laflamme and knocked him down. He then turned on Laflamme's assistant, Bill Bell, and tackled him. This action appalled NHL president Frank Calder, who suspended Couture from further play for life and fined him $100. Five years later, the life suspension was lifted, but Couture did not return to the NHL. He did play in another league, where he was soon in difficulty again after he hit an opponent over the head with a stick. In 1948, NHL president Clarence Campbell expelled for life Billy Taylor of the Rangers and Don Gallinger of the Bruins on charges of being associated with gamblers. At the time, Campbell stressed that no fix of any game was involved. The suspensions were not lifted until 1970 when both Taylor and Gallinger were middle-aged. In 1989, a life suspension was placed on Detroit's Bob Probert (charged with cocaine smuggling). It was later lifted. These are the most severe penalties ever handed out.

Did Leaf owner Conn Smythe once invade a penalty box to fight a player from the opposing team?

It was more an argument than a fight. On March 12, 1936, during a game between Toronto and Montreal played in Montreal, Sylvio Mantha, playing-coach of the Canadiens, was penalized. Smythe invaded the penalty box to give Mantha a verbal lashing. The referee, Mike Rodden, intervened, and Smythe grabbed him by the sweater. Smythe's coach, Dick Irvin, joined in the act and tried to punch Mantha with a wild swing. The league president, Frank Calder, was in attendance, and he, too, jumped into the penalty box in a peacekeeping role. So did Ernie Savard, a Canadiens' governor. It was an amazing sight: the league president, two NHL governors (Smythe and Savard), a referee, a coach and a playing-coach all embroiled in a penalty-box rumpus.

What was the story behind Conn Smythe of the Maple Leafs once accusing an opposing team of trying to gain an advantage by sabotaging the Leaf players' skates?

During the 1935–36 season, after a game in Montreal between the Maroons and the Leafs, Smythe charged that an attempt had been made to slow down the fleet Toronto players. Some villainous characters had supposedly spread sand around the visiting team's dressing room in Montreal in an effort to take the edge off the players' skates. Tommy Gorman, manager of the Maroons, was indignant. He stated that if any sand was on the floor of the dressing room it must have come from Smythe's own sand and gravel pits in Toronto!

Eddie Shore, one of hockey's greatest defensemen, almost killed a Toronto player in the thirties. Was it an accident?

Apparently. In December, 1933, Eddie Shore of the Boston Bruins, almost killed Toronto's fine stickhandler, Ace Bailey. It happened this way. The Bruins, playing at home, enjoyed a two-man advantage over the

Leafs at one point in the game. Bailey, killing the penalties, did some fancy stickhandling to kill time. Finally, Shore came up with the puck and began a rush. However, King Clancy of the Leafs knocked him down and Toronto was once again in control. Shore regained his feet, saw Bailey in front of him, and charged. He caught Bailey from behind and flipped him high in the air. Bailey's head hit the ice and he lay motionless, severely injured. Red Horner, skating to Bailey's aid, said something to Shore, who just grinned. So Horner knocked Shore unconscious with one punch. Bailey hovered between life and death for several days and after emergency surgery made a slow recovery. He pulled through but never played again. Two months later, a benefit game was arranged in Toronto between the Leafs and a team of NHL All-Stars. Bailey and Shore met for the first time since the incident. "I know Eddie never meant to hurt me," said Ace. "It was an accident." The two men embraced at center ice and the ovation that followed lasted several minutes.

What NHL general manager was asked to serve in a similar capacity with a major-league baseball team?

Sam Pollock. The Montreal general manager, a great fan of baseball, was approached by the Toronto Blue Jays to operate that team when the Jays were granted an American League franchise.

Has a long-term player in the NHL ever gone through his entire career without taking a penalty?

No, but among forwards and defensemen, former NHLer Val Fonteyne perhaps came the closest. He played 820 NHL regular season games with three different teams over 13 seasons and compiled a mere 26 minutes in penalties. Through a span of five seasons, he failed to take a single penalty and in four seasons he took a single minor each year. At the end of his career, in two full WHA seasons, he received only two minors. What makes Fonteyne's penalty totals so impressive is that he was primarily used as a penalty killer, a role that often leads to infractions because it requires a lot of stick-checking.

Stanley Cup Trivia

1. True or false? A Stanley Cup winner qualifies to have his name engraved on the Cup if he has played in 40 regular season games during the Cup-winning season, or if he has played in one playoff game.

2. The Detroit Red Wings won back-to-back Stanley Cups in 1997 and 1998, matching a feat accomplished earlier in the decade by what team?

3. If a team wins the first two games of the Stanley Cup finals, history shows its chances of winning the Cup are:
   a. over 50% b. over 70% c. over 90% d. 100%

4. There is nothing more exciting than overtime games in the Stanley Cup Playoffs. The longest overtime game ever played lasted into what period?
   a. the 4th b. the 5th c. the 6th d. the 7th

5. The shortest overtime game in playoff history lasted all of:
   a. 4 seconds b. 9 seconds c. 12 seconds d. 21 seconds

6. Scotty Bowman, with eight Cup victories, is tied with Toe Blake for the most Cup wins by a coach. Can you name the teams Bowman led to the Cup and the number of Cups he won with each club?

7. Who am I? Following the 1987 Cup finals won by Edmonton, I was the lucky guy who won the Conn Smythe Trophy as MVP. I became the seventh goalie, the third rookie and the fourth member of a losing team to win it.

8. In 1989, I became the 12th person to win the Cup as a player and a coach. As a coach, I did it at the Montreal Forum where no visiting team had ever captured the Cup. Who am I?

9. In 1992, two NHL teams established a remarkable record by winning 11 straight playoff games. Name the teams.

10. Name the NHL goalie who has appeared in more playoff games than any other. Is it:
a. Grant Fuhr b. Patrick Roy c. Billy Smith d. Curtis Joseph

11. My name is Hal Winkler. I retired as a goaltender in 1928. In 1929, my former team had my name engraved on the Stanley Cup—even though I didn't play a game for them that season. They said they did it because they liked me. Can you name the team that honored me?

12. This hockey tough guy was involved in a Stanley Cup series between Seattle and the Canadiens. During the series most of the players on both teams came down with the flu. The series was canceled after five games. The player died in hospital a few days later. Do you remember his name? And the year he passed away?

13. Defenseman Bill Barilko also died after a Stanley Cup final series. He was killed in a plane crash while on a fishing trip. Barilko scored the Cup-winning goal for his team in overtime in that series in '51. Can you name the teams involved?

14. I was a surprise starter in goal for the 1997 Stanley Cup champions. But it worked out well because my team won and I captured the Conn Smythe Trophy. Surely you know the team I played for. But how about naming another Cup-winning team I played for?

15. I played a lot of years in the Windy City without getting a sniff at the Stanley Cup. Then I was traded to Montreal where I broke my ankle late in the season. Unfortunately, I missed all of the 1993 finals but I still have my name engraved on the Cup. Who am I?

16. Cheevers is the name—Gerry Cheevers. I played on two Stanley Cup teams for Boston in '70 and '72. On both occasions my backup was a goalie who went on to coach and manage in the NHL. Can you name him?

17. My goaltending career ended prematurely when I got a stick in the eye—right through my mask. But I won back-to-back Conn Smythe Trophies in the seventies. Do you know my name?

Plagued by concussions, Paul Kariya, when healthy, is one of the most dangerous goal scorers in the league.

18. Yeah, yeah, it's me, Grapes. Best thing that ever happened to Canadian television. And the worst thing that ever happened to me as coach was getting caught with too many men on the ice back in '79. Cost me my job in Boston when Harry wouldn't forgive me. Trouble is, I can't remember what team we would have met in the finals that year if it weren't for that stupid mistake, if we'd beaten Montreal. Help me out, willya?

19. It's me again, Grapes. I'm tellin' yuh, I must be losing my marbles. Cause now I can't remember which Montreal player scored the overtime goal that put us out in '79. I know I had Gillie Gilbert in goal and it took a perfect shot from Guy Lafleur to beat him to tie the score after we were caught with too many men on the ice. But who the heck scored the winner for the Habs in overtime?

20. Just one more question from me, coach-of-the-year and all that. Talk about my bad memory. Years ago, in 1964–65 I think it was, the league introduced a new playoff trophy named after old Conn Smythe. I really liked the first winner but his name escapes me. I'd ask McLean but I don't think he was even born then. Gimme a hand, willya? Who was the first Conn Smythe Trophy winner?

Answers:
1. True, 2. Pittsburgh, 3. c. (92.3%), 4. 6th, 5. 9 seconds (Montreal's Brian Skrudland vs. Calgary, 6. Montreal (5), Pittsburgh (1) and Detroit, (2) 7. Ron Hextall, 8. Calgary coach Terry Crisp who won the Cup as a player with the Philadelphia Flyers, 9. Chicago Blackhawks and Pittsburgh Penguins, 10. Patrick Roy, 11. Boston, 12. Bad Joe Hall, 1919, 13. Toronto and Montreal, 14. Detroit, Calgary, 1989, 15. Denis Savard, 16. Ed Johnston, 17. Bernie Parent, 18. New York Rangers, 19. Yvon Lambert, 20. Jean Beliveau 1965.

Stanley Cup Quiz

1. True or false? No NHL team with a lower than .500 regular season record has ever won the Stanley Cup.

2. When the Montreal Canadiens set a record with five straight Stanley Cups in the fifties, who did they beat in the finals in their fifth Cup-winning year?

3. What teams were involved in the only Stanley Cup final series in which all games were decided in overtime?

4. On April 18, 1987, the New York Islanders met the Washington Capitals in game seven of the Patrick Division playoff series. How many overtime periods were played before the game ended? Who scored the winning goal?

5. Who was the player who gained fame for scoring a Cup-winning goal while playing on a broken leg?

6. What long-standing playoff jinx ended for the Boston Bruins in 1988?

7. Who scored the disputed goal in overtime that brought the Dallas Stars the Stanley Cup in 1999?

8. Two men share the record for coaching the most Stanley Cup winning teams. Can you name them?

9. Who holds the NHL record for most game-winning goals in Stanley Cup play?

10. Name the player who earned all three stars after a playoff game.

11. The 1971 Stanley Cup finals were highlighted by turbulence in the camp of Montreal, the eventual champion. The coach clashed verbally with his team's toughest player and the latter was benched. A star forward on the team called the coach "incompetent" and "the worst coach I ever played for." This player then scored two goals in the seventh game to help win the Cup.
    a. Who was the coach?
    b. Who did he bench?
    c. Who called him "incompetent"?

12. When this 1980s team captured the Stanley Cup, their victory was followed by a riot in their home city, thousands of miles away. Where did the riot take place? What Stanley Cup final did it follow?

13. In 1986, the Montreal Canadiens won their 23rd Stanley Cup, surpassing another great franchise in another sport for most championships won. Can you name the franchise?

14. In the 1975 Stanley Cup playoffs, what team staved off elimination more times than any other?

15. In 1981 an NHL coach wore a black patch over his eye as a good luck charm in the playoffs. Who was he?

Answers:

1. False. In 1937–38, the Chicago Blackhawks, with a regular season mark of 14–25–9, went on to win the Cup. In 1948–49, the Toronto Maple Leafs, with a 22–25–13 regular season record, captured Lord Stanley's basin.

2. Toronto. In the first round of the 1960 playoffs, the Canadiens swept past Chicago in four straight games. In the finals against Toronto, they remained undefeated, ousting the Leafs in four straight. Goalie Jacques Plante allowed only 11 goals in eight playoff games.

3. Toronto and Montreal. It was the 1951 final round and the Leafs defeated the Canadiens four games to one. Sid Smith, Ted Kennedy, Harry Watson and Bill Barilko scored the overtime winners for the Leafs. Rocket Richard scored in overtime to nail down the only Montreal victory.

4. The game, the longest in 44 years, was settled in the fourth overtime period when Pat LaFontaine scored for the Islanders at 68:47.

5. Bobby Baun of the Leafs. It happened on April 23, 1964, in Detroit. Baun was carried from the ice on a stretcher. He returned for the overtime, his broken ankle numbed with painkiller, and scored the winning goal for Toronto. Only after the Leafs won the Stanley Cup two nights later did he consent to have his leg x-rayed.

6. The spring of 1943 marked the beginning of one of hockey's strangest jinxes. From then until the spring of 1988 the Bruins failed to win a playoff series from the Montreal Canadiens. The jinx finally ended when the Bruins ousted the Habs four games to one in the Adams Division finals.

7. Brett Hull.

8. Toe Blake and Scotty Bowman with eight.

9. Rocket Richard scored 18 game-winners in Stanley Cup competition, six of them in overtime, and Wayne Gretzky with 24.

10. *Rocket Richard. It happened after a Stanley Cup playoff game at the Montreal Forum. Richard, only 22, scored all five goals for Montreal in a game against Toronto. Final score: Richard 5, Toronto 1. It's a record that still stands. After NHL games at the Forum, the three stars are honored and they usually take a bow. This night the standing-room-only crowd was able to give a continuous ovation. Star No. 1, Star No. 2, and Star No. 3—all Maurice Richard!*

11. *a. Al MacNeil. b. John Ferguson. c. Henri Richard.*

12. *In May, 1986, while the Habs were celebrating their Stanley Cup victory over the Calgary Flames at the Saddledome, their triumph triggered a riot in Montreal. Montrealers took to the streets and the victory party soon turned ugly. People overturned cars, broke windows and looted stores. They lit a bonfire in downtown Montreal, and when a fire truck arrived they attacked it. A riot squad eventually cleared the streets.*

13. *The New York Yankees.*

14. *In 1975, the New York Islanders stubbornly kept their Cup hopes alive time after time. They won the deciding game of their best-of-three preliminary series with the Rangers. Then they captured games four, five, six and seven in the quarterfinals after losing three straight to Pittsburgh. The Flyers whipped them three straight in the semi-finals, but the Isles came back to win games four, five and six before finally bowing out in game seven. Eight times during the playoffs they staved off elimination.*

15. *In 1981, the Minnesota North Stars met the Boston Bruins in a best-of-three playoff series. The North Stars had played 35 games in Boston without a win and coach Glen Sonmor was desperate. Before the series, he was contacted by a psychic, Amy Puckett, who told him she saw the North Stars winning in Boston with Sonmor (who'd lost an eye in a hockey accident) wearing a black eye patch. So the coach pulled on the patch and his team won 5–4, breaking the Boston Gardens' jinx. The patch stayed on for the rest of the series and the North Stars won three straight games, eliminating the Bruins. Then they ousted Buffalo four games to one and followed up by beating Calgary four games to two. The Islanders finally ended the Stars' Stanley Cup hopes in the finals, winning four games to one. Still, Sonmor's lucky eye patch helped the Stars win 12 of 19 playoff games.*

Daryl Sittler set a record for scoring in 1976 when he collected 10 points in a game against Boston.

Other Cup Capers

Has any one Stanley Cup celebration surpassed all the others?

When the Philadelphia Flyers became the first expansion team to win the Stanley Cup, with a 1–0 win over Boston in the spring of 1974, it touched off a celebration that was incredible. The next day an estimated two million fans jammed Broad Street where the Flyers' were honored with a huge ticker-tape parade. The crowds were so deep and pressed so close to the open convertibles that the cars could barely move. Bernie Parent made his teammates chuckle when he dashed from his car, raced to the nearest house, and asked permission to use the bathroom.

Did the Montreal Canadiens once play two teams for the Stanley Cup, even though they expected to play just one?

Yes. In 1924, the Canadiens defeated Ottawa in the final series for the NHL championship. Then, through a bizarre series of events resulting from a squabble between competing leagues in western Canada, both Calgary and Vancouver showed up in Montreal to play the Canadiens for the Stanley Cup. That didn't bother the Habs. They disposed of Vancouver in two games and then routed Calgary in another best-of-three series. Goalie Georges Vezina, who played despite a temperature of 101°F, allowed just six goals in six playoff games that spring.

How did several Red Wings players lose a hefty playoff bonus in 1988?

Red Wings coach Jacques Demers caught six players, among them Bob Probert, John Chabot and Darren Veitch, out partying long after curfew prior to the Wings' biggest game of the year—game five of the Campbell Conference final against Edmonton. The Wings lost the game 8–4 and were eliminated. As punishment, Detroit owner Mike Ilitch denied the six players a $16,000 bonus he had intended to give them, a gift matching the bonus they received from the league.

When did an American team first become eligible to play for the Stanley Cup?

In 1914–15, when the Pacific Coast Hockey Association switched the franchise in New Westminster, B.C., to Portland, Oregon. A year later, the

Portland Rosebuds became the first U.S. team to appear in a Stanley Cup playoff. They lost to the Montreal Canadiens, three games to two.

Was the very first Stanley Cup game a box-office success?

Definitely! Played in Montreal, in 1894, the game attracted 5,000 fans, most of whom stood on a raised platform surrounding the ice surface.

Did the NHL once hire backup goaltenders for the Stanley Cup playoffs and make them available to all teams?

In 1942, the NHL governors decided to employ three minor-league goalies for the playoffs on a standby basis. They received $50 per game to stand by and another $50 if they were called upon to substitute.

Which American team was the first to win the Stanley Cup?

In 1916–17, the year before the birth of the NHL, the Seattle Metropolitans won the Stanley Cup. Seattle beat the Montreal Canadiens three games to one. Bernie Morris was Seattle's biggest star with 14 goals in the series, six in one game.

Which team took just two years to win the Cup after joining the league through expansion?

The New York Rangers, who joined the NHL in the 1926–27 expansion, won the Stanley Cup in 1927–28.

Is it true that the Stanley Cup was once kicked into a canal?

It's a good story and it may even be true. The story has been told that a drunken member of the famous Ottawa Silver Seven, on a dare, once booted the Cup into the Rideau Canal. Fortunately, the canal was frozen over and the following morning members of the team returned and scrambled into the canal to retrieve the trophy.

Is it true that the Stanley Cup was once left on a Montreal street corner?

That's how the story goes, and it happened after the Montreal Canadiens won the Cup in 1924. The Canadiens, as champions, were honored at a victory party at the Windsor Hotel in Montreal. "Let's take the Cup up to Leo Dandurand's house, fill it up with champagne, and have ourselves a little party," suggested one member of the team. "Swell idea," said the other. So into Dandurand's car they piled and headed for his home. Along the way they had to stop to change a tire, and while repairs were being made, the Cup was unloaded and placed on the curb. Repairs finished, the players jumped back in the car and soon arrived at Dandurand's house. The champagne was uncorked and a call went out for the Cup. The Cup was missing. It had been left on the curb. Back into the car they piled and off they rushed to the place where the flat tire had interrupted their journey. There stood the Cup on the sidewalk, just where they had left it.

Is it true that the Stanley Cup once disappeared from the Hockey Hall of Fame under mysterious circumstances?

The Stanley Cup was removed under stealthy circumstances from the Hockey Hall of Fame, in Toronto's National Exhibition Park. Despite a modern burglar alarm, thieves stole the Cup on December 5, 1970, adding the Conn Smythe Trophy and the Bill Masterton Memorial Trophy to their loot bag for good measure. Police later recovered all the stolen items.

What were the circumstances leading up to coach Lester Patrick's famous stint in goal during a Stanley Cup playoff series?

It happened in 1928 during the second game of the finals. The Montreal Maroons took the opener 2–0. Lester Patrick of the Rangers had long since retired as an active player when his team skated out against the Maroons two nights later, yet he was soon to become the central figure in one of the most amazing sports performances ever.

After four minutes of play in the second period, Nels Stewart rifled a shot that caught goalie Lorne Chabot flush in the eye. Chabot was taken to hospital, and Patrick immediately asked Eddie Gerard, the manager of the Maroons, for permission to use Alex Connell, the great Ottawa goaltender, as a substitute. Gerard refused. Patrick then asked for Hugh McCormick from London in the Canadian Pro League, but again his request was turned down.

Patrick, fuming, then decided to put on the pads and play in the net himself. He had done the same thing on two or three occasions before, but never with so much at stake. The silver haired Patrick was 44 years old, and the fans alternately hooted and cheered when he shuffled onto the ice to take his warm-up shots. When play began, Patrick amazed the fans with his agility. Throughout the rest of the game and into overtime, he handled 18 shots and was beaten only once when Stewart scored on a rebound. At 7:05 of the first overtime period the Rangers broke through and scored. The exhausted Patrick, dripping with perspiration, was mobbed by his players and escorted to the dressing room.

It is strange but fitting that Patrick, who spent his whole life in hockey and made many outstanding contributions to the game, will always be remembered more for his play as a substitute Stanley Cup goaltender than for anything else he ever did. It was one of hockey's most electrifying occasions. The Rangers went on to win the series and the Cup.

How did Ken Doraty gain hockey fame?

Doraty was the central figure in one of the longest overtime games ever played. In the Stanley Cup semi-finals of 1933, Boston played Toronto. The fifth game, played on April 3 in Toronto, was scoreless after 60 minutes of play. It remained scoreless after the first overtime period. Then came a second, a third, a fourth and even a fifth overtime period. Team officials suggested a flip of a coin should decide the issue, or perhaps the goalies should be removed. Meanwhile, play carried on and in the sixth overtime period, little Ken Doraty of the Leafs took a pass from Andy Blair and raced in to score. It ended a game that lasted 164 minutes and 46 seconds.

When did Bill Barilko score his famous game-winning goal in the Stanley Cup finals and what were the details?

The date was April 21, 1951; the scene, Maple Leaf Gardens in Toronto. The Leafs faced Montreal in game five, leading the series 3–1. All games had been won in overtime and the clincher was no exception. With Montreal leading 2–1, Joe Primeau, Leafs' coach, pulled his goalie and Tod Sloan scored with 32 seconds left to force another overtime. Then, after 2:53 of extra play, Bill Barilko took a pass from Howie Meeker and slammed the puck past Gerry McNeil in the Montreal net. It was Barilko's first point of the series and his last ever as a player. In August of that year, he and a friend, Dr. Henry Hudson, went on a fishing trip in the doctor's plane. They were never seen again. The wreckage of the plane was discovered in the early sixties.

The Gretzky File

When Wayne Gretzky retired on the final day of the 1998–99 NHL season, he left behind a multitude of records and accomplishments. With this quiz, lets find out how much you know about the greatest player ever to play the game.

1. Gretzky holds the record for most career goals with
    a. 894 b. 896 c. 898

2. Gretzky holds the record for most career points with
    a. 2,500 b. 2,750 c. 2,857

3   How many Stanley Cup teams did Gretzky play on?
    a. four b. five c. six

4. In 1981–82 Gretzky scored 50 goals in the fewest number of games (from the start of a season). He scored them in
    a. 40 games b. 39 games c. 38 games

5. The only team Gretzky played on without scoring a single goal was
    a. Toronto Marlboros b. Peterborough Petes c. Barrie Flyers

6. When Gretzky broke Gordie Howe's record for most career points (1,850) in 1989 what team was he playing for
    a. Edmonton b. St. Louis c. Los Angeles

7. Wayne's brother Brent was an NHLer for 13 games with Tampa Bay, where he became part of one of hockey's highest scoring brother acts. How many NHL goals did Brent score
    a. one b. ten c. twenty

8. On the day after Gretzky retired he and his Ranger mates took part in another sport. Was it
    a. badminton b. golf c. bowling

9. Gretzky says his biggest thrill in hockey was
    a. scoring his first NHL goal b. winning his first Stanley Cup c. his first Hart Trophy

10. In 1978, before he signed with Edmonton, he played with a pro team in
    a. Winnipeg b. Birmingham c. Indianapolis

Answers:
*1. 894, 2. 2,857, 3. Four, 4. 39 games, 5. Peterborough Petes (He played 3
games with the Petes in 1976–77 and collected 3 assists), 6. Los Angeles,
7. One, 8. Bowling, 9. His first Cup, 10. Indianapolis of the WHA.*

Did You Know?

If Wayne Gretzky had never scored a goal in the NHL he would still hold
the record as the league's all-time highest scorer on the basis of his
1,963 assists. He collected 113 more assists than Gordie Howe had total
points.

High Scoring Families

Hockey is a family affair. There have been many high scoring families in
the NHL—the Howes, the Hulls, the Sutters and the Richards. Your
job—and this is a tough one—is to match the goal totals below with the
families who scored them. When you're finished, you'll have listed the
top five goal scoring families.

Family goal totals: 1499, 1314, 1003, 902, 895 and 821

Family: Howes: Gordie, Mark, Marty and Vic
         Hulls: Bobby, Dennis, Brett
         Sutters: Brian, Darryl, Duane, Brent, Rich and Ron
         Gretzkys: Wayne and Brent
         Mahovlichs: Frank and Peter
         Richards: Maurice and Henri

Answers:

The top five list should look like this: **Total goals**

1. **The Hulls: Bobby (610), Dennis (303), Brett (586)** — 1499
2. **The Sutters: Brian (303), Brent (363), Darryl (161),** — 1314
   Duane, (139) Ron (199) and Rich (149)
3. **The Howes: Gordie (801), Vic (3), Mark (197) and Marty (2)** — 1003
4. **The Richards: Maurice (544) Henri (358)** — 902
5. **The Gretzkys: Wayne (894), Brent (1)** — 895

The next five families on the list would appear in the following order:

6. **The Stastnys: Peter (450), Anton (252) and Marian (121)** — 823
7. **The Mahovlichs: Frank (533), Peter (288)** — 821
8. **The Dionnes: Marcel (731) and Gilbert (61)** — 792
9. **The Mullens: Joey (502) and Brian (260)** — 762
10. **The Espositos: Phil (717) and Tony (0)** — 717

Wait. Here's More.

Just for fun, here are more questions about goal scoring families. Who scored more NHL career goals:

1. Don Cherry or his brother Dick?

2. Charlie Conacher or his brother Roy?

3. Syl Apps Sr. or Syl Apps, Jr?

4. Sylvain Turgeon or his brother Pierre?

5. Geoff Courtnall or his brother Russ?

Answers:

1. Dick Cherry outscored Don 12–0, 2. Roy Conacher outscored Charlie 226 to 225, 3. Syl Apps Sr. outscored Syl Jr. 201 to 183, 4. Pierre Turgeon has outscored Sylvain 397 to 269, 5. Geoff Courtnall has outscored Russ 365 to 297 (as of 1998–99).

Rookie Goal Scorers

1. I'll name some NHL players who enjoyed outstanding rookie
    seasons. Your job is to recall the number of goals they scored as
    freshmen. Choose one of the three numbers next to their names.

Rookies		Goals scored		
Teemu Selanne (1992–93)	_____	66	76	86
Mike Bossy (1977–78)	_____	53	54	55
Mario Lemieux (1984–85)	_____	45	44	43
Joe Nieuwendyk (1987–88)	_____	51	61	41
Dale Hawerchuk (1981–82)	_____	45	46	47
Luc Robitaille (1986–87)	_____	45	46	47
Rick Martin (1971–72)	_____	46	45	44
Steve Larmer (1982–83)	_____	43	44	45
Barry Pederson (1981–82)	_____	44	45	46

2. Only two players on the above list failed to win the Calder Trophy.
    Can you name them?

3. Only one of the players on the above list failed to better his rookie
    goal scoring mark in succeeding seasons. Who is he?

4. Name the player on the above list who went on to score a career-
    high 85 goals in a season.

5. Name the player above who holds the NHL record for total points by
    a rookie.

6. What is the NHL record for most points by a rookie? Is it:
    a. 132 points b. 130 points c. 128 points

7. Because he played in the WHA in 1978–79, Wayne Gretzky was not
    eligible for the Calder trophy when he joined Edmonton the
    following season. Had he been eligible, his first year NHL points
    total would have made him the top all time rookie scorer. How many
    points did he collect?
    a. 133 b. 135 c. 137

8. Gretzky's first year goals total would have placed him in a tie with one of the players on the above list. Which one?

9. Only five rookies have scored 100 or more points in a season. Can you name three of them?

10. The top three rookie points leaders played with clubs that are no longer in the NHL. Can you name the players and their first-year teams?

Answers:

1. *Selanne 76, Bossy 53, Lemieux 43, Nieuwendyk 51, Hawerchuk 45, Robitaille 45, Martin 44, Larmer 43, Pederson 44.*
2. *Rick Martin and Barry Pederson*
3. *Teemu Selanne*
4. *Mario Lemieux*
5. *Teemu Selanne*
6. *132 points*
7. *137 points*
8. *Joe Nieuwendyk, both with 51*
9. *Teemu Selanne, Peter Stastny, Dale Hawerchuk, Joe Juneau, Mario Lemieux*
10. *Selanne (Winnipeg), P. Stastny (Quebec) and Hawerchuk (Winnipeg)*

All-Time Sinners

Dave "Tiger" Williams was a favorite with Toronto fans in the seventies. But he spent a lot of time in the penalty box—over 60 hours! Tiger is the all-time sinner. He tops the list for career penalty minutes with 3,966, an average of 4.12 minutes per game. Your job is to match the penalty minute totals below with the player who compiled them. Then we'll have a list of the top five NHL bad men.

Minutes Served: 3,565   3,146   3,319   3,043

Player: Chris Nilan   Tim Hunter   Marty McSorley   Dale Hunter

1.   Tiger Williams   3,966
2.   _____   _____
3.   _____   _____
4.   _____   _____
5.   _____   _____

The correct list should look like this:

1. **Tiger Williams**   **3,966**
2. **Dale Hunter**   **3,565**
3. **Tim Hunter**   **3,146**
4. **Marty McSorley**   **3,319**
5. **Chris Nilan**   **3,043**

The Top Goalies

Brian's compiling a list of the NHL's six winningest goaltenders. He needs your help in placing the correct number of career wins opposite each goalie's name.

Career Wins: 434   447   423   412   407

Winningest goalies: Glenn Hall, Terry Sawchuk, Patrick Roy, Tony Esposito, Jacques Plante

	Goalie	Wins
1.	_____	_____
2.	_____	_____
3.	_____	_____
4.	_____	_____
5.	_____	_____

The List should look like this:

1. **Terry Sawchuk**   **447**
2. **Jacques Plante**   **434**
3. **Tony Esposito**   **423**
4. **Patrick Roy**   **412**
5. **Glenn Hall**   **407**

Great Goal Scorers

All of the following have scored over 500 career goals. Can you identify them?

1. This player who scored 507 career goals was once approached about serving as Canada's Governor General.

2. He's the career scoring leader among U.S.-born players with 502 goals.

3. He's the top goal scorer among European players with 601 goals.

4. He's the top Montreal-born goal scorer with 613 goals.

5. He scored 573 goals in just 10 seasons and with just one team.

6. He's scored 586 goals, as of 1998–99 but his father scored 610.

7. As of 1998–99, he's scored 592 goals. But the team record is 786, set by Mr. Hockey.

8. He's the only NHLer to score exactly 500 career goals.

9. He was the first player to score 500 goals. He finished his career with 544.

10. He scored 731 career goals playing with the Red Wings, Kings and Rangers.

Answers:
1. *Jean Beliveau*
2. *Joe Mullen*
3. *Jari Kurri*
4. *Mario Lemieux*
5. *Mike Bossy*
6. *Brett Hull*
7. *Steve Yzerman*
8. *Lanny McDonald*
9. *Maurice Richard*
10. *Marcel Dionne*

The NHL's Assist Leaders

Only five active NHL players have cracked the 1,000 assist mark in their careers. Wayne Gretzky tops the list with 1,963. Brian needs help in placing the next four assist leaders on a list. Match the number of assists below with the players named and you'll have the top five in the assists department.

Career assists: 1,963   1,050   1,037   1,102   1,083

Players: Wayne Gretzky, Mark Messier, Ron Francis, Paul Coffey,
           Ray Bourque

	Player	No. of assists
1.	Wayne Gretzky	1,963
2.	_____	_____
3.	_____	_____
4.	_____	_____
5.	_____	_____

Your list should look like this
1.	Wayne Gretzky	1,963
2.	Paul Coffey	1,102
3.	Ray Bourque	1,083
4.	Mark Messier	1,050
5.	Roy Francis	1,037

Guess How Many

Note: Measurements from the *NHL Guide and Record* book are listed in feet and inches.

1.   How many fans attend NHL games each year?
     a. over 12 million b. over 15 million c. over 18 million d. over 22 million.

2.   A hockey puck is _____ inches thick and _____ inches in circumference.

3.   How many games combined do all the teams play in one NHL season?
     a. 1,066 b. 1,166 c. 1,266 d. 2,066

4. How many teams were in the NHL during 1998–99?
   a. 24 b. 25 c. 26 d. 27

5. How many teams will be playing in the NHL by 2000–2001?

6. How many feet are there from the goal line to the end boards behind the net?
   a. 13 feet b. 4 feet c. 18 feet d. 12 feet

7. How many referees are there in the NHL? (1998–99 season)
   a. between 20–25 b. between 30–35 c. between 40–45 d. between 60–70

8. How many Presidents or Commissioners have governed the NHL since its inception in 1917?
   a. 15 b. 10 c. 7 d. 6

9. Under NHL rules, what's the maximum number of inches in the length of a hockey stick?
   a. 55 b. 58 c. 63 d. 65

10. How many players (including goaltenders) are allowed to dress for a game in the NHL?
    a. 18 b. 20. c. 22 d. 24

11. How many miles (approximately) does a referee skate during a game (one-referee system)?
    a. 5 b. 7 c. 9

12. Coming into the 1998–99 NHL season, goaltenders had faced 625 penalty shots (since the rule was introduced in 1934–35). What percentage of penalty shots have they stopped?
    a. 40% b. 50% c. 60%

13. In 1998–99, Canadian-born players made up the majority of the NHL rosters (slightly more than 60%). Making up almost 24% of the rosters were players from
    a. the U.S. b Europe

14. The Montreal Wanderers played in the NHL for part of the league's initial season in 1917–18. Then their arena burned down and they disbanded. Before leaving, they won just one game, their home opener, by a lop-sided score over Toronto. Was the score
a. 10–9 b. 10–0 c. 10–2

15. In a game in New York on January 10, 1935, the official scorer awarded a record number of assists on a goal by Toronto's Joe Primeau. How many assists could he possibly have awarded?
a. 2 b. 3 c. 4

Answers:
1. c., 2. one inch by three inches, 3. a. 1,107, 4. 27, 5. 30, 6. a. 13 feet, 7. d. (60–70), 8. 6 (Calder, Dutton, Campbell, Ziegler, Stein and Commissioner Bettman), 9. c. 63, 10. b. 20., 11. c. 9, 12. c. slightly over 60%, 13. Europe (23.9%), 14. 10–9, 15. c. 4.

General Knowledge Quiz

1. Name the only coach to win back-to-back Stanley Cups with two different teams. Clue: It happened in the thirties.

2. Who was the oldest rookie ever to play in the NHL?

3. Who is the only player to win at least eight Stanley Cups and not make it to the Hockey Hall of Fame?

4. What was the most lop-sided win in Olympic hockey history?

5. When was the last time a goalie played without wearing a mask and when was the last time a player was allowed to play without wearing a helmet?

6. Who was Hobey Baker?

7. When was the first game between two U.S. colleges played?

8. Has a U.S. college hockey team ever gone through a season undefeated?

9. When did the Zamboni ice-resurfacing machine make its NHL debut?

10. Who was the first player to score 50 goals in a season while performing for two NHL clubs?

Answers:

1. *Tommy Gorman, Chicago Blackhawks in 1934, Montreal Maroons in 1935.*

2. *In 1973, the St. Louis Blues signed veteran defenseman Connie Madigan who made his NHL debut late in the 1972–73 season at age 38. Madigan played in 20 games and collected three assists.*

3. *Montreal's Claude Provost.*

4. *In 1924 at Chamonix, the Toronto Granites represented Canada at the Olympics. The Granites whipped Czechoslovakia 30–0, Sweden 22–0 and Switzerland 33–0 in the preliminary round. They went on to rout Great Britain 19–2 and the U.S. 6–1 in the final round. Canada won the gold medal outscoring the opposition 110–3 in five games.*

5. *Goalie Andy Brown, who played his final season with Pittsburgh in 1973–74, became the last NHL goaltender to play without a mask. In 1979, all players entering the NHL were required to wear helmets but those in the league prior to that season had the option of going bare-headed. Craig MacTavish, who played his final season with St. Louis in 1996–97, was the last player to play without a helmet.*

6. *Hobey Baker was a great hockey star at Princeton shortly after the turn of the last century and was said to be on a par with the best Canadian players of that era. He was killed in a plane crash at the end of World War 1. He is a member of the Hockey Hall of Fame, a rare honor for a U.S. amateur player.*

7. *On Feb. 1, 1896, Yale University played Johns Hopkins. Two years later, on January 19, 1898, Brown defeated Harvard in the first college game between two schools still involved in the sport.*

8. *Yes. In 1969–70 Cornell produced an unbeaten, untied record of 29–0–0 for coach Ned Harkness. This team was named the best U.S. college team ever.*

9. *On March 10, 1955, Toronto played at Montreal but most of the attention during the game was on the Zamboni ice-cleaning machine which was employed for the first time at an NHL game.*

10. *Craig Simpson, who started his third NHL season with Pittsburgh, was traded to Edmonton on November 24, 1987. He scored 13 goals as a Penguin that season and another 43 as an Oiler to become the only player to score 50 plus goals with two clubs in the same season. It was his only 50-goal season.*

Do You Know Your Hockey History?

When was artificial ice invented?

Experiments with artificial ice began over a century ago. In England, in 1876, scientists mixed glycerine with water, chilled it with ether, and circulated it through copper pipes covered by water to produce a frozen surface. The first artificial ice rink in the United States was installed in old Madison Square Garden in New York in 1879. It covered 6,000 square feet. Hundreds of skaters turned out on opening night, February 12. Artificial ice rinks did not appear in Canada until 1911, when rinks in Vancouver and Victoria installed the necessary equipment.

When did women first begin playing organized hockey?

Women have been playing the game almost as long as men have. In 1894, and possibly even earlier, women's teams were matched against each other at McGill University in Montreal. There is a photo in the National Archives in Ottawa of Lady Isobel Stanley, Lord Stanley's daughter, playing hockey with some friends on the outdoor rink at Government House in 1890.

Who is credited with devising the helpful signals that referees use to denote infractions?

Bill Chadwick, the New York–born referee and Hall-of-Famer, deserves credit. He devised the hand signals that have made the game more understandable. Chadwick retired in 1955.

Hockey once employed seven men on each team. What were the positions called?

Goal, point, coverpoint, rover and three forwards. Point and coverpoint were the defensemen who played one behind the other. The rover, as the name implies, roamed at will on the ice. He was the key man, usually the fastest skater and the most skilled. On the attack, he rushed; on defence, he fell back. The position disappeared from hockey in eastern Canada in 1911 but continued in the West until 1922. It was dropped strictly as an economic move because it was less expensive to ice six men than seven. In 1911–12, the National Hockey Association, forerunner to the NHL, elected to play with six men per side. The Pacific

Coast Hockey Association went to six men in 1922, a year after the newly formed Western Canada Hockey League began in 1921 with six per side.

When did goal nets first make their appearance in hockey?

In 1899, a hockey fan, Frank Nelson, dreamed up the idea while watching Australian fishermen cast their nets. He brought two nets home with him and showed them to W.A. Hewitt, then sports editor of the *Montreal Herald*. Hewitt persuaded the Montreal Shamrocks and the Montreal Victorias to try the nets in an exhibition game. Nets came into general use in 1900.

How talented were the Ottawa Silver Seven?

We go back to the years 1903 through 1906 to track down the record of this amazing team. In three seasons, the Silver Seven (originally composed of seven Ottawa natives) played in nine Stanley Cup series and won 17 of 20 Cup matches.

When did hockey players begin wearing numerals on their uniforms?

Players were first required to add large numbers to their jerseys under a new ruling by the NHA in 1912. The numbers with the players' names were listed on a large board at rinkside. This identification system eventually led to printed programs with names and numbers included.

Did goal judges once stand out on the ice and signal a goal by waving a hand in the air?

Yes, they did. From before the turn of the century into the 1920s, a goal judge took his place directly behind the goal and made his decisions from that risky position. He waved a hand or a handkerchief if the puck crossed the goal line. He was often bowled over by players racing in behind the net and if the referee thought he was a biased official, he could be (and often was) replaced by a spectator called out of the crowd.

Has a hockey team ever gone on strike?

Yes. In the spring of 1925, the Hamilton Tigers enjoyed the best record of any team in the NHL. As league champions, they drew a bye in the playoffs and would meet the winners of the Toronto-Montreal series.

However, team captain Wilf "Shorty" Green (Red's brother), a Hamilton star, claimed that the Hamilton players had performed in more games than was called for in their contracts. As a result, the players voted not to take part in the playoffs unless more money was forthcoming. When the players refused to budge in their demands, league president Frank Calder suspended and fined them. He declared that the winner of the Montreal-Toronto series would be league champion. The Canadiens won that series, but then lost the Cup in a playoff with Victoria, the WCHL champion.

Calder subsequently announced that the Hamilton franchise would be sold to New York interests and the city of Hamilton's only chance to win the Stanley Cup went by the boards.

Why was the 1928–29 season called "The Year of the Shutout"?

One man scored a record number of shutouts in the 1928–29 season, hence the name. Diminutive George Hainsworth of the Canadiens, over the course of the 44-game schedule, blanked the opposition in no less than 22 games. No player has come close to that mark since. Perhaps no player ever will.

The Philadelphia Flyers joined the NHL in the 1967 expansion. Were the Flyers the first team to represent the City of Brotherly Love in the NHL?

No. The Pittsburgh Pirates, who won five games in the 1929–30 season, shifted their franchise to Philadelphia in 1930–31. As the Quakers, they were operated by former prize fighter Benny Leonard but lasted only one season before folding, winning four games and tying four games for a record low 12 points. The club lost $100,000 of the backers' money.

How did the Chicago Blackhawks get their name?

When the NHL expanded into the U.S. market in the 1920s, Major Frederic McLaughlin acquired the Chicago franchise. He brought in the Portland Rosebuds team and renamed it for the Black Hawk artillery division, in which he had served during World War I. The division, in turn, had honored the name of Chief Black Hawk, famed Illinois Indian leader. In 1985 the club changed the name from Black hawks to Blackhawks.

When was the longest overtime game played and which teams were involved?

On March 24–25, 1936 (yes, it spanned two days), Detroit played the

Montreal Maroons in the Forum. The teams played the equivalent of three games, from 8:34 p.m. to 2:25 a.m., before the winning goal was scored by Detroit's Modere (Mud) Bruneteau against Montreal goaltender Lorne Chabot. The goal was scored at 16:30 of the sixth overtime period, after 116 minutes and 30 seconds of overtime play. By the time Bruneteau scored to win the game, the players hadn't eaten for almost 12 hours. The late Jack Adams, who coached the Red Wings, recalled, "And by George, they were too tired to eat after it was all over."

The box score of this longest game offers an interesting sidelight. Only one penalty was called through the six overtime periods. Oddly, it was called against the Detroit goalie, Norm Smith. The referees were Ag Smith and Bill Stewart. "They just didn't want to call anything," Adams explained.

What caused the memorable riot at the Montreal Forum in 1955?

The riot stemmed from a suspension Clarence Campbell levied against Montreal star Rocket Richard after a game in Boston on March 13. Richard had attacked Hal Laycoe with his stick and punched a linesman, Cliff Thompson. An angry Clarence Campbell suspended Richard for the final three games of the regular season (costing him a chance to win his first and only scoring title) and all of the playoffs. On March 17, despite threats and warnings, Campbell attended a game at the Forum between Montreal and Detroit. One young fan approached Campbell and threw a punch at him. He was pelted with eggs and tomatoes. Suddenly a tear-gas bomb exploded on the ice and the game was terminated. The building was cleared and panic, which could have led to disaster, was narrowly averted. Outside, thugs and looters took over and roamed along St. Catherine Street, ripping through stores, smashing car and store windows. The riot caused thousands of dollars' damage and resulted in numerous arrests. Campbell, spirited out of the Forum, was fortunate to escape alive.

What were the details of the hockey scandal involving a game timekeeper in the NHL?

During the 1960s in Montreal it was discovered that a game timekeeper appeared to be letting a precious second or two slip by on the clock after a goal was scored. An investigation revealed that, influenced by a betting syndicate, the fellow was attempting to stop the clock at certain seconds. In many cities, heavy betting is made on the time of goals, the time of the final goal, and so on. Manipulation of the clock for a second or two could mean big winnings for the gamblers.

Has an NHL game ever been forfeited?

Yes. Tommy Gorman, who coached the Black hawks to a Stanley Cup in 1934, once became so incensed over a ruling by referee Bill Stewart that he pulled his players off the ice. Stewart gave Gorman one minute to get them back on again. When Gorman refused, Stewart dropped the puck at center ice. Cooney Weiland of Boston skated in and fired the puck in the net. The game was forfeited and it went into the books as a 1–0 Boston victory. On March 17, 1955, a game in Montreal between the Canadiens and the Red Wings was forfeited to Detroit following the famous St. Patrick's Day Riot. On February 27, 1926, Toronto (trailing 4–3 to Montreal) forfeited the game when Toronto's Babe Dye refused to give the referee the puck.

Was betting on hockey games prevalent early in the century?

Wagers were frequent and often large—especially on games played in the mining towns. In 1898 an Ottawa newspaper, stating that "everyone makes predictions and wagers as to the outcome of matters," conceived a plan whereby all readers of the sports page had an opportunity to show just how correctly they could pick the results of games. The entire hockey schedule was printed and the paper generously agreed to reward the person who could predict the winners of every game with a sum of five dollars.

Hockey Lingo

1. A point is awarded to a player who takes part in a play leading up to a goal by a teammate. The point is called an _____.

2. Forwards come back into their own zone to protect their goalkeeper. They call it _____.

3. A fake or feint by a puck carrier attempting to skate around an opponent or the opposing goalie is called a _____.

4. A player scoring three goals in a game is credited with a
   _____.

5. Pinning the puck up against the boards with either a stick or a skate
   to stop play is called _____ the puck.

6. Shooting the puck the length of the ice from your own zone when
   both sides are even is called _____ the puck.

7. When a player breaks out and has no one to beat but the goalie, he
   is said to be on a _____.

8. In the final minute of a game, the team trailing by a goal often tries
   this strategy. It's called _____.

9. When the puck is passed forward to a teammate on the move the
   play is called _____ the puck.

10. The most common types of shots are the _____ and the
    _____.

Answers:

1. assist
2. back-checking
3. deke
4. hat trick
5. freezing
6. icing
7. breakaway
8. pulling the goalie
9. head-manning
10. slap shot and wrist shot

Do You Really Know Hockey?

1. One of these men has not been president of the NHL.
   a. Clarence Campbell b. Frank Calder
   c. Lester Patrick d. Red Dutton e. John Ziegler

2. One of these players never scored 60 goals in a season.
   a. Mike Bossy b. Jari Kurri c. Phil Esposito d. Mario Lemieux e. Rick
   Vaive

3. One of these players never played 20 or more seasons in the NHL.
   a. Johnny Bucyk b. Norm Ullman c. Stan Mikita d. Jean Ratelle e. Rod Gilbert

4. One of these players failed to score 100 points in his rookie season.
   a. Dale Hawerchuk b. Peter Stastny c. Mike Bossy d. Mario Lemieux

5. One of these coaches has won more games with the same team than any other coach in history.
   a. Billy Reay b. Dick Irvin c. Scotty Bowman d. Al Arbour

6. One of these trophies is not awarded to an NHL player.
   a. Norris Trophy b. Art Ross Trophy c. Calder Cup d. Conn Smythe Trophy e. Hart Trophy

7. One of these players was not a first overall selection in the entry draft.
   a. Mario Lemieux b. Pierre Turgeon
   c. Denis Savard d. Wendel Clark e. Joe Murphy

8. One of these teams reached the Stanley Cup finals in the eighties.
   a. St. Louis b. Minnesota c. Washington d. Detroit e. Toronto

9. One of these lines never played in the NHL.
   a. Pony Line b. Punch Line c. Kraut Line.
   d. Telephone Line e. GAG Line

10. One of these players never scored over 500 career goals in the NHL.
    a. Gilbert Perreault b. Jean Beliveau
    c. Norm Ullman d. Frank Mahovlich e. Johnny Bucyk

Answers:

1. *c,* *2. e,* *3. e,* *4. c,*

5. *d (Bowman has more total wins than Arbour but he compiled them with five different teams.) Arbour with 739 wins with the Islanders. Bowman has the most total wins.*

6. *c (The Calder Cup is an American League trophy sometimes confused with the Calder Memorial Trophy.)*

7. *c (Denis Savard was picked third behind Doug Wickenheiser and David Babych in the 1980 entry draft.)*

8. b (Minnesota reached the finals in 1981 and lost to the Islanders.)
9. d (We've never heard of the Telephone Line.)
10. c (Ullman came close to 500 goals—with 490 for his NHL career.)

Figure It Out

How does the NHL calculate a goaltender's goals-against average?

Take the goals against, multiply by 60, and divide by the total minutes played. If a goalie plays 2,345 minutes over the course of a season and has 78 goals scored against him, multiply 78 by 60 and you get 4,680. Then divide 4,680 by 2,345 and you come up with 1.99. That's a great average for any goaltender.

How does one figure out a team's power-play efficiency?

Take the number of attempts with a man advantage (even if there is only one second of advantage time, it counts as an attempt) and divide that number into the number of power-play goals scored. In 1988–89, the Leafs had the NHL's worst power-play with 56 goals scored on 334 attempts. Divide 56 by 334 and you get a dismal power-play percentage of 16.8.

How do you figure a team's penalty-killing efficiency?

Take the number of times a team is shorthanded (same criteria as for power-play attempts) and subtract the number of power-play goals allowed. Then divide that number by the number of times the team played shorthanded. In 1988, Calgary was shorthanded 457 times. The Flames allowed 78 goals while at a disadvantage. Divide 379 by 457 and you get a penalty killing percentage of 82.9—best in the league.

How do you determine a team's winning percentage?

Take the team's total points (wins are worth two points, a tie one point). Then divide by the number of actual points a team could have won (games played multiplied by two). In 1988–89, Calgary led the NHL in points with 117 out of a possible 160 points. Divide 117 by 160 and you get a winning percentage of .731.

Pittsburgh led the NHL in team penalties in 1988–89 with an average of over 33 minutes per game. How did league statisticians arrive at this figure?

They took the Penguins' total penalty minutes (including bench minutes) and divided that figure by the number of games played. With 2,670 minutes in 80 games, the Penguins had a whopping team penalty average of 33.4.

How do you figure a player's plus-minus rating?

A player receives a "plus" every time he is on the ice when his team scores an even-strength (not necessarily full-strength) or shorthanded goal. A player receives a "minus" each time he is on the ice when his team allows an even-strength or shorthanded goal. Power-play goals do not count in either case. The number of pluses are balanced against the minuses to determine the total.

Who Wore What?

Match the star player with the original number he wore in the NHL.

1. Rocket Richard   a. 5
2. Gordie Howe   b. 17
3. Bobby Hull   c. 16
4. Marcel Dionne   d. 15

Answers:
1. d. 15, 2. b. 17, 3. c. 16, 4. a. 5

Who Remembers the Birth of the WHA?

In the early seventies, making the World Hockey Association a success was no easy task. Some of the things that happened were unbelievable. Let's test your memory with this true or false test.

1. The founders of the WHA were Dennis Murphy and Gary Davidson.

2. One of the original franchises was from Miami—the Screaming Eagles.

3. A franchise was awarded to Dayton, Ohio.

4. It cost each new owner $1 million to buy a franchise.

5. The first WHA player draft held in California was so professionally handled it even amazed Alan Eagleson, an onlooker.

6. Goalie Mike Curran, former star of the U.S. Olympic team, was the first player to sign a standard WHA contract.

7. Wayne Connelly and George Gardner were the first two NHL players to sign with the new league.

8. Bobby Hull signed a $2.75 million contract with Winnipeg and the next day scored six goals for the Jets.

9. Combined losses by the WHA in its first season were estimated at $10 million and no team made money.

10. The Miami Screaming Eagles begat the Philadelphia Blazers who begat the Vancouver Blazers.

11. Philadelphia's home opener was canceled when the Zamboni crashed through the thin ice, prompting hundreds of fans to throw souvenir pucks at the team owner.

12. The Ottawa Nationals quickly ran out of money and moved to Toronto, where they became the Toros.

13. The league president promised the WHA would begin play in 1972–73 with 12 teams; it would attract players from all calibre of leagues; and it would have parity of competition. All three promises were kept.

14. Although Winnipeg signed Bobby Hull, other owners had to put up money to help pay his salary.

15. Cincinnati liked the WHA so much investors there paid $1 million to join.

Name the Coach

1. Who was the youngest coach in NHL history?
   a. Gary Green b. Michel Bergeron c. Ted Sator d. Brian Sutter

2. Who was the oldest coach in NHL history?
   a. Lynn Patrick b. Toe Blake c. Dick Irvin d. King Clancy

3. The unprecedented move (through the courts) to block the suspension of this coach during the 1988 playoffs led to a wildcat strike by game officials. Who was the coach involved?

4. Which Ranger coach once ordered his players to practice immediately after a game as punishment for a losing effort?

5. In the Campbell Conference finals of 1986, this crafty coach was caught throwing pennies on the ice to force some illegal time-outs. Can you name him?

6. Who was the last player-coach in the NHL?
   a. Doug Harvey b. Red Kelly c. Charlie Burns d. Dick Irvin

7. In his first two seasons as a coach in the NHL, his team finished first overall in the league standings. It's an impressive record for:
   a. Glen Sather b. Terry Crisp c. Mike Keenan d. Pat Burns

8. He's the first coach in NHL history to win 40 or more games in each of his first three seasons.
   a. Al Arbour b. Terry Crisp c. Mike Keenan d. Jacques Demers

9. He coached the Leafs to five Stanley Cups, including three in a row in the forties.
   a. Dick Irvin b. Hap Day c. Joe Primeau d. Conn Smythe

10. In 1981–82 he took the last-place Jets from 21st place to 10th, a remarkable one-season improvement. A few months later he was fired.

a. Tom McVie b. Barry Long c. Tom Watt d. Bill Sutherland

Answers:

1. *b. Bergeron coached Quebec when he was 34 years old. Gary Green coached Washington at age 26.*

2. *d. King Clancy coached his last game with Toronto when he was 69 years old. Lynn Patrick and Dick Irvin were both 63 when they bowed out.*

3. *Jim Schoenfeld, who had been suspended for making derogatory remarks about referee Don Koharski.*

4. *a. Phil Watson. In the fifties, after a loss to the Montreal Canadiens late in the season, Watson shocked his team with the order: "Get back on the ice!" He then proceeded to put his players through a gruelling practice. Such a thing couldn't happen today. The NHL Players' Association wouldn't permit it.*

5. *Jacques Demers.*

6. *c. Charlie Burns was a player-coach for the North Stars during the final 18 games of the 1969–70 season and for six playoff games. Burns succeeded Wren Blair as coach on December 28, 1969, but did not play in the first 26 games he coached.*

7. *b. Terry Crisp.*

8. *c. Mike Keenan. His Philadelphia Flyers won 53, 53, and 46 games in his first three seasons there.*

9. *b. Hap Day.*

10. *c. Tom Watt.*

Team Nicknames

1. The New York Rangers, founded in 1926, were called the Rangers because:
   a. Their owner was from Texas and liked the name Texas Rangers.
   b. The owner was a fan of the Lone Ranger.
   c. The owner's wife, former showgirl Rose Marie Ranger, suggested it.

2. The Detroit Red Wings earned their nickname because:
   a. The owner's wife liked red-winged blackbirds.
   b. The owner envisioned his players flying down the ice.
   c. The owner borrowed the name from a Montreal team called the Winged Wheelers.

3. The Pittsburgh players are called Penguins because:
   a. They are hardy creatures who look good on ice.
   b. The name was the result of a "Name the Team" contest.
   c. The name was borrowed from a local amateur team named the Penguins.

4. The Toronto players are called Maple Leafs because:
   a. The maple tree grows everywhere in Toronto.
   b. Owner Conn Smythe, a patriot, thought it fitting his team should wear the same maple-leaf emblem his troops wore in WW I.
   c. The name came with the franchise when Smythe bought the team.

5. The Calgary franchise is known as the Flames because:
   a. The team hoped to become the hottest thing on ice.
   b. It had something to do with Alberta Oil.
   c. It relates to the city of Atlanta burning to the ground during the Civil War.

6. The New Jersey team adopted the name Devils because:
   a. The owner said he "had a devil of a time" buying the Colorado Rockies and moving them to New Jersey.
   b. The name was inspired by a demonic creature once said to terrorize New Jersey.
   c. The name came to the owner in a dream.

Answers:
1. a, 2. c, 3. b, 4. b, 5. c, 6. b.

Rules and Regulations

How is a goal determined?

The puck must cross completely over the red goal line, either along the ice or into the area below the crossbar. In other words, the puck may be three-quarters of the way inside the goal but will not constitute a score.

If a puck hits the goalpost, is it considered a shot on goal?

No. The NHL reasons that the shot wasn't good enough to score, so it ought not to count as a shot on goal.

If the puck bounces off a player and into the net, is it a shot on goal?

Yes, but if the shot is deflected off an opposing player and into the net, the shot on goal is credited to the player taking the shot. If it deflects off a teammate and goes in, the teammate is given credit for the shot.

If the puck strikes an official and is deflected into the net, does it count as a goal?

No. The goal would not be allowed.

If a team pulls its goaltender on a delayed penalty, can a goal possibly be scored against that team?

Yes, if the puck is accidentally shot, pushed or deflected into the empty goal by a player on the non-offending team.

Why do referees allow goals to count after they were seemingly kicked into the goal by an attacking player?

This is a judgement call by the referee. If the ref feels there was no deliberate attempt to kick or direct the puck into the goal, he'll allow the score to stand.

If a goalie, in catching the puck, brings his catching hand in back of the goal line, is it ruled a goal?

Yes. If the goal judge sees the goalie's glove, with the puck in it, completely across the goal line, he should signal the goal.

Can a goalkeeper be evicted from a game?

Yes, when he has incurred three major penalties.

Are there any occasions when a player may continue to play with a broken stick?

Yes. A goalie may play with a broken stick, but he is the only player allowed to do so. What's more, a teammate may take the goalie a new stick while play goes right on.

On a penalty shot, must the goalkeeper stay in his crease or can he come out to meet the shooter?

The goalie must stay in his crease until the shooter touches the puck. Then he may move out and challenge the shooter if he wishes. In the event he moves away from the crease before the shooter touches the puck, the shot will be allowed. If a goal results, it counts. If the shooter misses, he is awarded a second penalty shot.

Are NHL goalkeepers allowed to captain their own teams?

No. It is thought that goalkeepers would take too much time plodding up the ice to protest decisions. In the past, goalkeepers sometimes were captains, an example being Bill Durnan of Montreal.

What significant change was made in the penalty-shot rule for the 1938–39 NHL season?

For the first time the player taking the penalty shot was allowed to skate right in on the goaltender. Previously the player had to shoot from behind a line on the ice and remain behind the line after shooting.

When is a penalty shot imposed?

When a player with control of the puck in the attack zone, and with no other opponent to pass except the goalkeeper, is tripped or fouled from behind. Other infractions that call for a penalty shot include the following: when a player, other than the goalkeeper, deliberately falls on the puck in the area of the goal crease or picks up the puck from the goal crease area; when a player on the defending side, including the goalkeeper, coach, manager or trainer, throws a stick or other object at the puck in his defending zone.

When is "icing the puck" not an infraction?

When:
a. the opposition goalie touches the puck first, or it crosses through the crease,
b. an opponent is able to play the puck before it crosses the goal line,
c. the team shooting the puck is short-handed due to a player in the penalty box,
d. a teammate who is not offside touches the puck first,
e. the puck touches an opponent before crossing the goal line.

Hockey's Funny Rules

Why does hockey have an "icing the puck" rule?

There's an interesting story behind this regulation. In the thirties, the New York Americans were playing the Boston Bruins in Boston. The Bruins had a powerful team and the Americans discovered that one way to keep Boston off the scoresheet was to lift the puck down the ice at every opportunity. Bruins' manager Art Ross figured the Americans "iced the puck" 87 times during the game and he was furious. He vowed to give the Americans a taste of their own medicine when the teams met back in Madison Square Garden. In the return match, the Bruins "iced the puck" exactly 87 times. The fans, of course, were the losers. They were rocked to sleep by the long, aimless shots down the ice.

The NHL governors soon took steps to see that such a farce didn't happen again. They slapped a rule in the book that deterred, if not prevented, a team from lifting the puck down the ice at will.

When a player serves a penalty for the goaltender on the team, who is credited with the penalty minutes?

The goaltender. All penalties charged to a goalkeeper, regardless of who serves time in the box, are reflected in his statistics.

What are the dimensions and weight of the puck? Why are they frozen before games?

The puck is three inches in diameter and one inch thick. It is made of vulcanized rubber and weighs between five-and-a-half and six ounces. Pucks are frozen before NHL games so that they won't bounce too much.

What did the old-time rule about "sitting on the fence" refer to?

At the turn of the century, when a referee ordered a player to "sit on the fence" it meant he was penalized. If there was no penalty box the player would sit on the low boards surrounding the rink until the referee allowed him back in the game.

When were goaltenders first allowed to leave their feet to block shots?

Prior to the formation of the NHL in 1917, goaltenders in the National Hockey Association who fell to the ice to block shots could be penalized and subjected to a fine of two dollars. In the Pacific Coast Hockey Association, a professional league founded by Frank and Lester Patrick in 1911, goalers were permitted to flop or leave their feet from the beginning.

When were all of a team's players first required to sit on the bench? Why?

In 1921, the NHL ruled that all players must sit on the bench during games. Prior to that, on bitterly cold nights, substitute players (starters often played the full 60 minutes) would sit in the dressing room, warming themselves around a stove and passing the time by playing cards and telling stories. In Ottawa one night, the coach, using a buzzer system, buzzed for King Clancy to come out and play. But Clancy had his skates off. By the time he was ready to play, the crowd was restless and the referee was angry. So the NHL ruled that all players, in future, must remain on the bench. They, of course, became known as "benchwarmers."

When was it ruled that a team could have only one goalie on the ice? Why?

In 1931, the NHL ruled that no team may play more than one goaltender on the ice. Previous to this ruling, in at least one playoff game, a team tried to thwart a more powerful team by placing two goaltenders in the net at the same time. The strategy didn't work, though, because the two goalies bumped into each other and got in each other's way.

Each goalie has a crease, but does the referee also have one?

Yes. The referee's crease is a semi-circular area marked on the ice (ten feet in radius) directly in front of the penalty bench. It's designed to keep hot-tempered players away from the officials when penalties are called or when discussions among the officials are warranted.

If a player is delayed in getting to the arena because of a car accident or bad weather, and the game is under way when he arrives, is he allowed to play in the game?

No. A list of names and numbers of all eligible players must be handed to the referee or official scorer before the game, and no change shall be permitted after the commencement of the game.

If a player is knocked unconscious during a game, why do some referees allow the play to continue while others, in similar circumstances, will blow the whistle immediately?

Under the rules, play shall not be stopped when a player is injured until the injured player's team has possession of the puck. Hence the delayed whistle. If, however, the injured player's team has possession of the puck at the time of the injury, play shall be stopped immediately, unless his team is in a position to score a goal.

Does the official scorer sit next to the penalty timekeeper so that he'll be able to hear the referee and record the goals and assists?

No. The official scorer is generally in an elevated position in the arena with telephone access to the public address announcer. The official scorer decides who gets credit for goals and assists and his decision is final. The referee merely reports the name or number of the player scoring a goal. He does not deal with assists.

What's a commonly broken rule that goes unpenalized?

Rule 68(b) states: "Players shall not use profane language on the ice or anywhere in the rink before, during or after a game. For violation of this rule, a misconduct penalty shall be imposed except when the violation occurs in the vicinity of the players' bench in which case a bench minor penalty shall be imposed."

Most players are totally unaware that profane language is banned anywhere in the rink, which, of course, includes the team dressing room before, during, and after each game.

Rules in Review

1. Coach Clunker thought he spotted an opposing player using an illegal stick, so he had his captain call for a measurement. But the referee ruled the stick was perfectly legal. Does he penalize coach Clunker's team?

2. True or false? On a face-off in an end zone, both players facing off must place their sticks in the designated face-off area at exactly the same time.

3.   Gary the goalie ran a truck over his goal pads, flattening them so that they were three inches wider than NHL's legal limit. But Gary was caught in a random inspection and was penalized. Was he given:
     a.   a minor penalty
     b.   a one-game suspension
     c.   a 10-game suspension

4.   Crazy Cole is furious when the referee penalizes him for high sticking. He grabs the ref by the shirt, pushes him up against the boards, and shakes him. Then he cools off, pulls himself together, and apologizes. The referee should:
     a.   give Cole a minor penalty.
     b.   give him a game misconduct (which carries an automatic supension of at least three games).
     c.   give him a major penalty.
     d.   forgive and forget.

5.   Oh, oh. Gary the goalie has broken his stick. What's this? A teammate has thrown Gary a new stick from the bench. But the referee won't let Gary use it. He stops play and:
     a.   gives Gary a minor penalty.
     b.   gives the opposing team a penalty shot.
     c.   gives Gary's team a bench minor.
     d.   makes Gary use part of his broken stick until the next whistle.

6.   There are seconds left in the game and the home team needs a breather, so Gary the goalie deliberately displaces the net, forcing a break in the action. But the referee catches Gary and orders a penalty shot. The player taking the shot is selected by:
     a.   the referee from any player on the non-offending team.
     b.   the captain of the non-offending team, from any of his team mates on the ice when the foul occurred.
     c.   the coach of the non-offending team from any of his players.

7.   Puckhog Perkins has a huge curve in the blade of his stick and the opposing team demands a measurement. But Puckhog outsmarts them. He steps on the blade and cracks it in two before the referee can measure it. The referee:
     a.   throws Puckhog out of the game.

   b.   gives Puckhog a minor penalty.

   c.   gives Puckhog a minor penalty plus a 10-minute misconduct penalty.

   d.   makes Puckhog glue the stick back together again.

8.   Goalie Hextall has a wonderful opportunity to score another goal. All the opposing players are caught in behind his net where they've fallen down. So Hextall lugs the puck down the ice, outskating everybody. But the referee blows his whistle, stopping Hextall's breakaway. He gives Hextall a minor penalty. Why?

9.   Hotshot Harry needs one more point to win the scoring race. In the final game he thinks he earned an assist on a goal, but the official scorer doesn't give it to him. The next morning Harry phones the scorer and complains. The scorer replies:

   a.   "Harry, I'll check the videotape and get back to you."

   b.   "If you tell me honestly you earned the point I'll give it to you, Harry."

   c.   "Harry, it's too late for a change. The request had to be made at the end of the game last night."

   d.   "Put your request in writing and send it to Gary Bettman."

10.   The referee and both linesmen have food poisoning and can't work the game. The managers of the teams can't agree on substitute officials. Under the rules, they decide to:

   a.   postpone the game.

   b.   select a player from each team to officiate, with the home team player acting as referee.

   c.   put on skates and officiate themselves.

   d.   have the team assistant coaches do the job.

11.   Coach Clunker has another trick up his sleeve. His team is tired and he wants a time-out, but he's already used his official timeout. Thinking quickly, he tosses some pennies on the ice and directs the referee's attention to the coins. But the referee has seen Clunker heave the coins and tells him:

   a.   "That'll cost you a bench minor, Clunker."

   b.   "You're out of the game, Clunker, and I'm keeping the money."

   c.   "You're going to be fined and suspended now, Clunker. I'm telling the commissioner on you."

d. "Just for that I'm giving the opposing team a penalty shot, Clunker."

12. Now Coach Clunker's in trouble with his team's owner. During the warmup before the game last night, Clunker's players started a fight with the opposing team. Clunker's boss moans:
   a. "That little brawl is going to cost the team $25,000 in fines."
   b. "Teams that fight before the game lose their first-round draft choices."
   c. "Coaches of teams involved in pre-game fights are automatically suspended for a year, Clunker. So pack your bags."
   d. "If you'll apologize to the league president and the opposing coach we may get out of this without a penalty, Clunker."

13. Tony loves hockey and soccer. During a hockey game he kicks the puck toward the opponent's goal. The puck takes off, bounces off the crossbar, hits an opposing defenseman in the back and trickles into the net. The referee says:
   a. "Nice try, Tony, but no kicking allowed in this game. No goal!"
   b. "It's a weird goal, Tony, but it counts."
   c. "Two minutes for kicking, Tony."
   d. "No goal. Face-off in the corner."

14. Bad Bart has been brawling and the referee orders him to the dressing room. But Bad Bart comes back from the dressing room to his team's bench to collect his stick and gloves. That's when he shouts a few words at the game officials. The referee spots him and tells him:
   a. "That's going to cost you, my boy. A game misconduct and an automatic suspension, 10 games with no pay."
   b. "That's it. I'm awarding the game and two points to the opposing team."
   c. "You have 30 seconds to collect your gear and get out of here."
   d. "Any more nonsense from you and I'll have you barred for life."

15. Just when Breakaway Bob was racing down the ice with the puck, some fool threw another puck on the ice. Bob kept going and scored

Dominik "The Dominator" Hasek dominated the net as well as the Vezina trophy race for much of the 1990s.

a goal. The opposing team howled. They wanted to know why the referee didn't stop the play when the second puck appeared. He explained:

a. "What! And spoil Bob's chance for a goal?"
b. "There's nothing in the rule book to cover such a thing."
c. "The rule says I can't stop play until there's a change of possession."
d. "I thought the linesman was going to pick up the second puck."

Answers:

1. **Yes. He gives Clunker's team a bench minor penalty since the stick did not violate the rules. Clunker's team is also fined $100.**
2. **False. The visiting player must place his stick within the designated area first.**
3. **b. Gary is given a one-game suspension.**
4. **b. Cole gets a game misconduct. He also draws an automatic 20-game suspension for applying physical force to the official.**
5. **a. Gary is given a minor penalty.**
6. **b. The captain of the non-offending team, from any of his teammates on the ice.**
7. **c. The referee gives Puckhog a minor penalty and a ten-minute misconduct. Puckhog will also be fined $200.**
8. **Once goalie Hextall crossed the center red line he broke a rule. Goalies are not allowed to participate in a play beyond center ice. A minor penalty results.**
9. **c. "Harry, it's too late for a change." No requests for any changes in any award of points shall be considered unless they are made at or before the conclusion of actual play in a game by the team captain.**
10. **b. Select a player from each team to officiate with the home team player acting as referee. When two of the three game officials were late arriving in Hartford a few years ago, two players, Mickey Volcan and Garry Howatt, acted as game officials until the second period.**
11. **a. It's a bench minor for Clunker.**
12. **a. The little brawl is going to cost the team an automatic $25,000.**
13. **b. Tony's unorthodox kick shot paid off. It's a goal. But only because it deflected in off the back of the defenseman. A straight kick shot of the puck into the net is not allowed.**
14. **a. Bad Bart got a game misconduct and a 10-game suspension without pay.**
15. **c. The rule says the referee can't stop the play unless there's a change of possession. Bob's goal counts.**

So You Think You Know Hockey?

Try these questions selected from a questionnaire used at a referees' school.

1. What kind of penalty does a player risk if he persists in banging his stick against the boards?

2. What is he assessed, if anything, when he receives a third major penalty in a game?

3. Does a goaltender who is assessed a third major penalty in a game receive an additional penalty?

4. If a penalty-shot attempt fails, where is the puck faced off?

5. Is a player allowed to push the puck along the ice with his hands?

6. If the puck strikes an official in the attacking zone so as to create an advantage to the attacking team, is play stopped?

7. A player causes the puck carrier to be distracted when he shoots part of a broken stick in his path. Should a penalty be called?

8. A second puck appears on the ice. Is play halted immediately?

9. A goalkeeper receives a misconduct penalty. Who serves the penalty?

10. The puck mysteriously breaks in two pieces. One piece enters the net. Is it a goal?

Answers:

1. *He risks a misconduct penalty.*
2. *He receives a game misconduct penalty.*
3. *He receives a game misconduct penalty. A substitute goalie takes over.*
4. *On a corner face-off spot in the zone in which the attempt was made.*
5. *As long as he does not deliberately pass it to a teammate. He can pass in his defensive zone (behind blueline).*

6. **Yes.**
7. **Yes. He receives an interference penalty.**
8. **Not necessarily. Play may continue with the original puck until there is a change of possession.**
9. **It must be served by a teammate who was on the ice at the time of the infraction.**
10. **No. The complete puck must cross the goal line for it to count as a goal.**

Overseas

Which nation holds the record for the most lopsided victories in Olympic competition?

Canada. The Toronto Granites, winners of the Allan Cup in 1922 and 1923, represented Canada at the 1924 Olympics in Chamonix, France, and their record was astonishing. The Granites walloped Czechoslovakia 30–0, Sweden 22–0 and Switzerland 33–0. In the game against Switzerland, the Canadian team scored 14 goals in the 3rd period alone, a rate of nearly one a minute. In the preliminary round, the Granites' record was 85 goals for, none against. In the finals, Canada beat Britain 19–2, and the U.S. 6–1. In five matches, the Granites amassed 110 goals and allowed just three. These records have never been approached.

In what year did two hockey teams representing the same country show up for the Olympic Games?

In 1948. In January of 1948, two teams from the U.S. showed up for the Olympics in St. Moritz, Switzerland. One team, managed by Walter Brown of the Boston Bruins, represented the Amateur Hockey Association of the United States. Another represented the Amateur Athletic Union. Avery Brundage, president of the U.S. Olympic Committee and a rising power in international sports, supported the AAU bid and blasted the AHAUS team as being "professional." Brundage was over-ruled and the AHAUS team was permitted to play. The AAU team sportingly cheered their compatriots on in the games that followed but Brundage, when he walked in the pre-Olympic parade, was pelted with snowballs by the spectators.

Who won the first world championship meeting between Canada and the Soviet Union in 1954?

The Soviet Union. In their first-ever participation in the world hockey championships at Stockholm, Sweden, the Soviet team beat Finland 7–1, Norway 7–0, Germany 6–2, Czechoslovakia 5–2 and Switzerland 4–2. When they tied Sweden 1–1 the title rested on their game with Canada. Canada's team, the East York Lyndhursts, had outscored their opposition 57–5. The Soviets, paced by the brilliant play of Vsevolod Bobrov, beat Canada 7–2 to become world champions in their very first attempt.

When Team Canada played the Soviet Union in the famous 1972 series, did some Canadian players desert the team and return home?

Yes. Vic Hadfield, who'd scored 50 goals for the Rangers the previous season, was unhappy with his role on Team Canada and decided to return to Canada before the four games in the Soviet Union got underway. Rick Martin of the Buffalo Sabres was the next to bow out when Team Canada coaches wouldn't guarantee him playing time in the last four games. Jocelyn Guevremont of Vancouver quit for the same reason and Gil Perreault of Buffalo joined his buddy Rick Martin to make it a four-player walkout.

World Hockey Quiz

1. The International Ice Hockey Association Hall of Fame is located in what city:
    a. Helsinki b. Berlin c. London d. Las Vegas

2. A player born in Helsinki is the NHL's all-time leader in scoring among players born outside of North America. Who is he?

3. The U.S. and Canada were favored to win the gold medal at the 1998 Winter Olympics at Nagano, Japan. Both finished out of the medals. Which country won gold?

4. The sister of a well-known NHL star was the captain of the U.S. women's hockey team at the Nagano Olympics. Can you name her?

5. In the past four decades, the U.S. has won two Olympic gold medals in men's hockey. Can you name the two years they reigned as champs?

6. In what two resort centers did the U.S. win Olympic gold medals?

7. In 1951, a team from Western Canada won all six of its games in the World Hockey Championships in Paris, outscoring the opposition 62–6. Was this team the:
    a. Trail Smoke Eaters b. Penticton V's c. Lethbridge Maple Leafs

8. The largest audience at any hockey game, pro or amateur, turned out for the final match of the 1957 World Championships between the USSR and Sweden at the Grand Sports Arena in Moscow. The attendance was a reported:
    a. 30,000 b. 40,000 c. 50,000

9. The Whitby Dunlops won the World hockey title in 1958 in Oslo by outscoring the opposition 82–6 and defeating the USSR in the final game 4–2. The captain of the Dunnies was a defenseman who went on to coach and manage in the NHL. Can you name him?

10. The Dunnies recruited a former star Toronto Maple Leaf captain to help them win the 1958 World Championship. Can you name this former Lady Byng Trophy winner?

Answers:
1. Helsinki, 2. Jari Kurri, 3. The Czech Republic, 4. Cammi Granato, 5. 1960 and 1980, 6. 1960 Squaw Valley, 1980 Lake Placid, 7. Lethbridge Maple Leafs, 8. 50,000, 9. Boston's Harry Sinden, 10. Sid Smith.

ONe TiMe TrOPhY WiNNers

The following players or coaches won a major NHL trophy only once. I'll name the winner and the year he was recognized. You name the award.

1. Ted Nolan, 1997
2. Claude Lemieux, 1995
3. Randy Carlyle, 1981

4. Ron Francis, 1995
5. Eric Lindros, 1995
6. Michael Peca, 1997
7. Ed Belfour, 1993
8. Brett Hull, 1991
9. Jim Carey, 1996
10. Don Cherry, 1976
11. Mike Vernon, 1997
12. Mats Naslund, 1988
13. Marcel Dionne, 1980

Answers:

1. Jack Adams, 2. Conn Smythe, 3. Norris, 4. Frank Selke, 5. Hart, 6. Frank Selke, 7. Vezina, 8. Hart, 9. Vezina, 10. Jack Adams, 11. Conn Smythe, 12. Lady Byng, 13. Art Ross.

More On-Ice Oddities

1. You may not believe this, but a player named Vic Ripley once led his NHL team in scoring with 11 goals and 2 assists for 13 points. And that was for 34 games. Runner-up in team scoring was Johnny Gottselig with 8 points in 44 games. Can you tell me what impotent franchise they played for?

2. In 1995–96 a NHL team held a little-known record. It was their 29th consecutive season with a winning record, the longest such streak in any of the professional sports. Want a clue? It was an Original Six team but not Montreal. Name the team.

3. A team didn't need two goalies when this man played. He was an ironman, the last NHL goalie to play every minute of the season (70 games) in 1963–64. Who was this durable puckstopper?

4. It sounds impossible but this player did it—on New Year's Eve, 1988. He scored five goals in a game against New Jersey and each goal was different. He scored an even strength, a power play, a short-handed, a penalty shot and an empty net goal. Who was this puck magician?

5. Can you imagine a Stanley Cup game in which a player on one club played every position on the ice—including goal? It happened in a 1923 game. In that era, if a goalie was handed a penalty, he had to sit in the penalty box. In this game, an Ottawa player took over for him. He also played all the other positions. Do you know the name of this versatile chap?

6. What a horrible feeling. In a 1986 playoff game between Edmonton and Calgary, the score was tied 2–2 in game seven. A young Oiler defenseman celebrating his 23rd birthday tried a clearing pass from behind his team's net. The puck bounced off Grant Fuhr's skate and into the Edmonton net to give Calgary a 3–2 lead. There was no more scoring and the gaffe by the youngster became a part of Stanley Cup lore. Do you remember his name?

7. He lost more games (352) than any other nhl goaltender. But he won almost as many (335) and he played on four Stanley Cup champions, was a first team all-star in 1967–68 and he's in the Hockey Hall of Fame. Surely you know this unflappable fellow?

8. Who was the youngest goalie to play in the nhl? He broke in during the 1943–44 season.

9. In 1949, Toronto owner Conn Smythe ordered his pudgy goaltender to lose 7 of his 197 pounds—or else! The goalie's fast made headlines across Canada. People called it the "battle of the bulge." The player made the weight with ounces to spare. Who was he?

10. In a 1959 playoff game in Chicago, the fans disagreed with a famous referee's call. Three of them stormed on the ice and poured beer on the official. They knocked him to the ice. When the league president told a newspaperman the referee "choked" the angry official turned in his resignation. Who was the referee? What teams were competing?

11. Can you name the hockey player who turned down a fee of $75,000 to appear nude in a nationally known magazine? It happened in 1992.

12. Can you believe an exhibition game played in 1992 produced the largest crowd to see an NHL hockey match—25,581? I want you to tell me where the game was played?

13. Can you name the oldtime hockey player who wrestled bears in the off-season?

14. What was Kate Smith's association with the Philadelphia Flyers three decades ago?

15. Only Gordie Howe scored more career goals than this (now retired) right winger who enjoyed a streak of 15 consecutive 30-goal seasons. He finished his career with 708 goals but he never won a major award or a Stanley Cup. Can you name him?

Answers:

1. Chicago, 2. Boston, 3. Ed Johnston, 4. Mario Lemieux, 5. King Clancy, 6. Steve Smith, 7. Gump Worsley, 8. Harry Lumley was 17 years and 38 days old when he played for the Detroit Red Wings on Dec. 19, 1943. Moe Roberts, who played in only 10 NHL games, was 17 years and 363 days old when he made his debut with Boston on Dec. 11, 1925. 9. Turk Broda, 10. Red Storey in a game between Montreal and Chicago. 11. Female goaltender Manon Rheaume was asked to pose for Playboy. 12. St. Petersburg, Florida, in the Suncoast Dome. 13. Marcel Bonin was a 16-year-old hockey player when the circus came to Joliette, Quebec. Retired heavyweight champion Joe Louis, a circus employee, stood in a ring and challenged local strong men to wrestle a mean-looking brown bear he introduced, one that weighed about 400 pounds. Bonin eagerly jumped into the ring and fought the muzzled animal to a draw, earning a big round of applause. Bonin said, "I wrestled that old bear many times that summer, following the circus from town to town. What the people didn't know was that I went to visit the bear each morning and fed him and played with him. By the time I jumped into the ring he was happy to see me." Bonin went on to play 454 NHL games with Detroit, Boston and Montreal. 14. On December 11, 1969, aging singer Kate Smith's recording of "God Bless America" was played at the Spectrum in place of the national anthem. The Flyers beat the Leafs that night 6–3 and Kate's song became a good luck charm for the Flyers. When the team won back-to-back Stanley Cups in 1974 and '75, Miss Smith made three "live" appearances and the Flyers won all three times. Over the years her record wasn't perfect but it was mighty impressive. When she sang, the Flyers won 64 games and lost only nine. 15. Mike Gartner.